Winning People Over

14 Days to Power and Confidence

Winning People Over

14 Days to Power and Confidence

BURTON KAPLAN

Prentice Hall Press
Paramus, New Jersey 07652

Library of Congress Cataloging-in-Publication Data

Kaplan, Burton,
Winning people over : 14 days to power and confidence / Burton Kaplan.
p. cm.
Includes index.
ISBN 0-7352-0284-2 -- ISBN 0-13-315359-2 (cloth). -- ISBN 0-13-315227-8 (paper)
1. Interpersonal communication. 2. Interpersonal relations. 3. Success--Psychological aspects. I. Title.
BF637.C45K34 1996
158'.2--dc20 96-33660
CIP

© 1996, by Burton Kaplan
All rights reserved. No part of this book may be reproduced in any form or by any means without permission in writing from the publisher.

Printed in the United States of America

10 9 8 7 6 5 4 3 2 1

ISBN 0-7352-0284-2

ATTENTION: CORPORATIONS AND SCHOOLS
Prentice Hall books are available at quantity discounts with bulk purchase for educational, business, or sales promotional use. For information, please write to: Prentice Hall Special Sales, 420 Frisch Court, Paramus, NJ 07652. Please supply: title of book, ISBN, quantity, how the book will be used, date needed.

PRENTICE HALL PRESS
Paramus, NJ 07652

On the World Wide Web at http://www.phpress.com

Also by the Author

Everything You Need to Know to Talk Your Way to Success (Prentice Hall)

CONTENTS

Introduction

Everyone has an appetite for winning people over, and if you are one of them, this is a book you must own and read.

Written with busy people in mind, this is no ivory-tower exercise, no excursion in guesswork. Instead, these power-packed pages are the tested product of a 25-year program of study and research—solid, immediately practical techniques thousands upon thousands of America's most ambitious and capable men and women use daily to attain and hold the personal power and prestige their very livelihoods depend on.

Day by day these exciting pages help you with revealing self-tests, doable exercises, and step-by-step plans you can implement the moment you read them. Each of its hundreds of tips, techniques, procedures, and thumbnail case histories is the real thing. Every one of them is certain to help you make your fondest dreams come true. Together, they add up to a lifetime program—everything you need to:

> **Think with power and confidence:** The secrets of effective human relations enable you to take control of yourself, your business and personal relationships; steadily increase your value and importance to others, and get rid of the habits that silently rob your life of the joy you deserve.

Feel and act powerful and confident: To others we are what we appear to be. If we wish to be thought of as powerful and confident, we must look, dress, eat, talk, gesture, and speak accordingly.

Fourteen days to power and confidence: Each day is an easy-to-follow exercise in the successful resolution of a common issue of power and confidence most of us face daily.

Here is more than a book.

Here is the practical, immediately useful key to happiness that, until now, you could only dream about.

Burton Kaplan

PART ONE

AWAKEN THE POWER WITHIN

In this section you'll discover how to take charge of your life—how to think, feel, look, dress, and act in ways that empower you to take immediate and complete control of your business, personal, and social destiny. Here, you will discover how to develop the positive attitude you need to achieve success on the job, in the community, and at home; eliminate the hidden habits that rob you of happiness; clarify your goals and stand up for your opinions; put an end to shyness and self-consciousness; overcome the fear of failure; and find happy and fulfilling relationships.

Eight Ways to Avoid Failure and Achieve Success

Is there anyone, anywhere, who doesn't dream of being the hero of his or her own life?

Even the meekest and least worthy of us wants to believe, deep down, we have the power to touch and be touched in a special way. I am talking about the compelling power to create in others the desire to share our dreams and participate in our realities; to cure the heartache of shyness and the pain and suffering of low self-esteem; to overcome fear and build love; to solidify family relationships; to achieve the prestige of a corner office or the security of a successful business venture.

Most of us have had the humbling experience of seeing less worthy men and women achieve the personal recognition and financial rewards that seem to pass us by. Pained observers, we stand on the sidelines wanting to believe in our hearts the capacity for power and confidence are as much a part of our human potential as anyone else's.

How to Be the Master of Life Instead of its Victim

Twenty-five years ago, I made it my life's work to study the difference between people who made their dreams come true and the ones who somehow allowed their personal vision to get bogged down in the routines and frustrations of daily living.

I started with a fundamental belief in everybody's natural-born capacity to be the master and not the victim of their own lives. Why then, I wondered, do some of the least likely people end up with great personal power while others, with equal or better credentials, languish somewhere due south of their potential?

As a communication consultant to several of America's best-known organizations—Pepsi-Cola, Frito-Lay, Procter & Gamble, Revlon, and others—I worked closely with thousands of people. From Boston to Austin to Seattle, I observed the human traits and examined the human factors that set people up for success. What I conclude from years of research is a truth that is amazingly simple but exceedingly powerful when skillfully applied. Life has its winners and losers, but nobody's *born* a winner. You have to learn how to win. If you don't, you automatically train yourself to lose.

TEACH YOURSELF TO WIN

On the brighter side, my research also proves beyond reasonable doubt that losing doesn't have to be a life sentence. We aren't born ineffective. We train ourselves. So it figures: if we've trained ourselves, we can untrain ourselves. My first-hand studies convince me that it is never too late to restore the dream—to teach yourself to win. Time and again I've observed people in their twenties, thirties, forties, and even fifties lose and lose and lose . . . then win once and win it all.

I'll never forget the day it really hit me that a thrilling level of living is everybody's God-given birthright. I was interviewing Jean Pesin, 43. Long before I met her, Jean was a Chicago word processor in a dead-end situation.

> *"The miserable rut I was in was so deep it was a grave open at both ends," she reports. "I kvetched into the mirror about my frustrating boss. I complained privately about the incompetents who got promoted over me. I secretly tore my hair out over my let's-not-get-ahead-of-ourselves boyfriend. But I never had the confidence to confront them. I never said to any of them, 'Hey, in this life are a lot*

of things I have to take, but what you are doing to me isn't anything I need to swallow any more!'

"Can you imagine, to feel you don't have a right to be . . . well, to be your own person? Something had to give. I could not live with myself for another day if I didn't do something—anything!—about my life. I had to make something happen."

And she did.

Desperate for change, she finally turned off the mental tape that kept on saying, 'No matter what you do, it won't make any difference.'

Instead, Jean took steps to awaken and release the incredible but dormant power within. By immediately applying the proved and workable techniques you will learn in this book—tested, practical, step-by-step methods that have helped thousands of men and women create, live, and enjoy the life you dream of—she took complete control of the people, events, and circumstances that shaped her life, her career, her destiny!

Today, Jean is married. With her husband, Larry, 51, she owns and operates a thriving Chicagoland temp service. Her life is by no means perfect. But you should have seen the glow of satisfaction on her face when she told me that some of her best clients are the very people who once made her life seem like one long bad-hair day. "I used to feel that the people in my life were drawing a circle around me, and the circle kept getting smaller and smaller. Well, they still make circles. But now, I challenge the boundaries other people set and my life keeps on getting bigger and bigger."

I was so touched by her willingness to stand up to life's inevitable daily struggles, her ability to tap into her deepest strengths, and her unspoken understanding that if she didn't risk growing she was certain to face emotional death that I got choked up and at first couldn't speak. Think of it: Here was a successful woman who, just a few years earlier, lived a life whose dimensions were determined by others. Trapped in her fears and frailties, she stood whipped by circumstances, alone, despairing, paralyzed.

As I looked into her confident eyes and smiling face, it suddenly came to me: I realized that if Jean could muster the grace and determination to meet and master her helplessness, anybody could. After all, history is full of personal success stories—leaders like Moses and Jesus, heroes like Lincoln and Gandhi, and millions of otherwise ordinary folk who took the very same magnificently self-empowering steps she did. No, Jean was neither the first nor the only person to have rediscovered her essential self—a strong and growing self she continues to build even to this day. She didn't enjoy any special privilege from birth, didn't learn to get in touch with her strengths and overcome her doubt at some Ivy League college. I concluded that the inner power that liberated Jean's spirit and gave her life fresh meaning, purpose, and achievement, must be an essence asleep within us all.

HOW TO BECOME THE PERSON YOU WANT TO BE

Time has proved me right. Now, after a quarter century of closely monitored testing among professionals, teachers, business people, parents, lovers—people like you and me—I can speak with complete confidence. The same inspiring power available to my friend Jean Pesin is available to you. All it takes is the will to tap the deepest capacity that's within you, embrace it, claim it, make it your own.

True, awakening it is not something you jump out of bed and just do. Unless you happen to be born perfect, it takes effort to work on yourself and grow, to correct the weaknesses and develop the combination of skills, attitudes, and personal character that add up to a winning way of life. After all, you cannot possibly become what you wish to be by remaining what you are.

People sometimes think that making the kinds of changes Jean made amounts to emotional boot camp. Well, it isn't exactly dancing school. But I want you to know it is the quickest way to realize just how special you truly are; the best way to make your dreams come true; the surest way to acquire the shining inner strength that adds luster to your life and the lives of those around you—even if you are now very shy, on the quiet side, or simply not the social success you dream of being.

THE SECRET OF EVERY SUCCESSFUL PERSON

All of us want to close the gap between our dreams and our realities, to experience the thrill of knowing we have the power to make things happen in ways that make us feel useful to, and cherished by, ourselves and others. But, like Jean, our hopes prove to be our fears. We are so used to going through life ineffective, we can't seem to figure out how to make our future what it ought to be. Most of all, we fail to see that our disappointments are almost never anybody else's fault. They are largely—in fact, entirely—our own doing, the result of failing to learn how to deal successfully with other people.

Research proves the point. Time and again, I found that the doctor or the lawyer or the manager who enjoys the greatest success in life is not necessarily the most intelligent or the most skilled. The salesperson who gets ahead isn't always the most attractive or the brainiest. The couples who are happiest are not usually the best looking or the richest.

No, my results show that the common denominator of success has less to do with good looks or wealth or technical skills or intellect than with the ability to take other people into account. At the risk of oversimplifying, let me sum up thousands of hours of practical, hands-on experience by saying that if you do not get what you want from others it is because you do not get along with others *successfully*.

Note the stress I place on the word *successfully*. Sure, you may get along. But do you get along successfully?

- Weaklings "get along" by dodging bullets.
- Human doormats "get along" by letting people walk all over them.
- Dictators "get along" by stepping on everyone.

These and other ways of "getting along" may appear normal, but that sort of normality is, in the end, really a mask. It disguises a fundamental inability to deal with others in ways that produce results that leave everyone's ego intact.

My point is this: Look for true personal power at home, on the job, or out in the community. You will certainly find men and women who have the knack of dealing with people in meaningful and enjoyable ways that bring personal satisfaction to all concerned.

HOW TO RECOGNIZE AND OVERCOME YOUR WORST ENEMY

In your search for personal confidence and the power it generates, your worst enemy isn't your worst enemy after all. No, you are up against a far tougher foe: Yourself.

We are the enemy—the ones who, time after time, do ourselves in. That is why it is so very important to see how you derail yourself. Only when you recognize and understand that the impact of your behavior causes people to respond to you in the ways that rob you of confidence and undermine power can you hope to find a way around your mistakes.

But understanding yourself is only half of the process. Doing something about it is the rest. Once you know what causes you to work against your own interests, you can use the eight practical prescriptions in this chapter to cure the condition. Getting rid of the problems you unconsciously put in your way automatically begins the transformation to the kind of life you desire and deserve by encouraging others to respect your wishes and defer to your needs.

You will gain the understanding you need to develop rewarding relationships at every level of life—with family, friends, colleagues, and customers. From this new-found confidence born of self-awareness will emerge the undeniable power to make your life all that you want it to be.

The Four Major Causes of Failure and How to Avoid Them

During the course of my research, which aimed to discover the psychological, physical, and social markers for human power and confidence, I was naturally concerned about the flip side—why people fail. I am not talking about the kind of failure where people are thrown out on the street. I am talking about something more subtle, a kind of personal derailment that somehow prevents the frog from turning into the prince.

You see, I believe that success or failure is in our own hands. No one arrives in life perfect. The way we avoid derailing ourselves is by seeing through the illusions we create, knowing our shortcomings, and recognizing the need to change or manage around our flaws.

The four reasons I identified may surprise you. None of these are my pet ideas about the difference between winning and losing in life. Rather, they have all stood the test of how you must deal with people to get what you want. So important are these I want to give them to you right now. But before I do, a word of caution: Do not be surprised if you find more than one of these in yourself. You see, we are all a mix; nobody is one hundred percent anything. Depending on circumstance, we can be bossy or shy, angry or docile, submissive or assertive. It is only natural to expose one side of ourselves while hiding another. In giving you my list, I am asking you to identify the predominant way you respond to life.

1. Arrogance
2. Political game-playing
3. Aggression
4. Unmanaged anger

ELIMINATE ARROGANCE AND GAIN STRENGTH

It is only human to always want something from others—anything from a raise in pay from your boss to the esteem of your family and friends. Love, sex, marriage, relationships, buying and selling, community life—no matter what the focus, your task is the same: To somehow convince others to give you what you want and hope for.

- If you are single, it might be a first date.
- If you are a parent, it might be extra teacher attention for your child.
- If you are in sales, it might be an order.
- If you are a buyer, it might be the best terms.
- If you are in management, it might be keeping your work group focused on your priorities.

- If you are working toward community leadership, it might be the votes of those you wish to lead.

Life is a group enterprise. Without teamwork there is no life. The continuing evolution of humankind, for instance, demands sexual and social cooperation. These life-sustaining interactions are far more important than the ability of any one individual to survive or even prevail. Arrogance, on the other hand—which I define as insensitivity to other people—works against life-affirming cooperation. Instead of drawing people into a common cause, it isolates individuals. Seen in this way, it may not be overly dramatic to suggest that arrogance is really a subtle form of emotional or social suicide. At the very least, its effects are similar. Remember the old song, "One is the loneliest number."

Why you find big stars in constellations

Arrogant men and women come in every size, shape, and color. They live in every city and suburb. They hold every job imaginable. They are the intelligent ones who know everything and tell more than they know; who think no one else is intelligent; who act as if they hold a patent on ideas and ways of being; and who operate on the basis that their lifestyle and beliefs are the be-all and end-all. Their minds don't listen to any idea different from their own. They don't learn how to improve their thoughts when they are on-target or drop them when they are way off. They don't know how to simply let things be.

Notwithstanding what I have said so far, I do not mean to suggest that in life there is no room for big stars, soaring individual performances, and strong belief in one's own ideas and views of things—or, for that matter, that life needs to be a kind of a "go along to get along" environment where the only way to make it is to suck up. Far from it; I believe the exact opposite is true. Big stars and exceptional performers add juice to life. But I also happen to believe that they have to know how to tailor their roles to fit life's larger goals. That's why they are so good at building constellations.

"You can't just avoid being arrogant, that's not enough," reports Sam Nance, a Denver newspaper executive. "You have to learn to work with others."

There's an interesting study that explains Sam's point. The University of Washington assembled two groups of people and told them they had survived a plane crash in the desert. They had to find some way to get back to safety. One of the groups was given general guidelines about desert survival, the other was not. Nevertheless, the untrained group did just as well as the trained one. The reason was that the untrained group worked as a team.

How to harness the power of teamwork

In your work life, community life, and family life you probably come into daily contact with stars—people with robust egos and star quality written all over them. They stand out in a crowd because they turn people on, not off. They know how to work with and through others.

The winners in any group of people are like the blades of a pair of shears. They're joined together so they cannot be separated, often moving in opposite directions, just as often coming together. And when they do come together, they are stronger than when they are apart, cutting through everything that comes between them.

Whether it is a family discussion, a company quota, or a community fund drive, people get what they want by working together. Said another way, if you can't build teamwork, you'll probably never develop the power to get all you want and wish for out of life.

The vexing question is, How? How do you walk the narrow path between the strong and often appropriate desire to believe in yourself, and the utterly human and unending need for the regard, respect, and affirmation of others?

Well, there is no certain key, no fail-safe road map to avoid arrogance on the one side and subservience on the other. Rather, the path is a dimly lit alleyway marked by signs written in braille—less a matter of seeing your way than of feeling it. The following practical prescriptions are sure to guide you.

PRACTICAL PRESCRIPTIONS FOR OVERCOMING ARROGANCE

℞1: Listen better.

Listen to what others say, not what you think in response to what they are saying. Put more of your attention on what they are groping with than what you can do about it or why your ideas might be superior. Show them, in your responses, that you get the picture they are trying to get across. For instance, when a friend says he is thinking of quitting his day job to open his own business, you say, "Sounds like you are willing to bet on your talent."

℞2: Empathize.

Persist in seeing things only from your own point of view and you will never get an accurate picture of how your behavior causes others to say and do the things they do. The idea is to look at your thoughts from their perspective, to try to experience why they might say what they say. Seeing people as they see themselves, viewing life from their vantage point as well as your own, forces you to shape your thoughts in ways they can accept and act on.

℞3: Find something—anything—useful in what others say.

The idea is to be more accepting of others. Acceptance does not equal agreement. It means allowing others to be themselves and not carbon copies of you. When you can accept something without necessarily agreeing with it, you relate to others as more of an equal. This makes people more willing to engage with you.

QUIT PLAYING POLITICS AND GAIN REAL POWER

Although it amounts to the moral equivalent of professional wrestling, some people choose the side of an issue by looking at who is on the other side. It happens at home, it happens on the job, and it happens out in the community. In fact, it can happen any time three or more people are linked by concerns of work, family, or common interest.

"My ex-friend, Debbie, is a politician. She will say or do whatever she thinks will help her get ahead," reports Anna-Louise Merriman, a Cincinnati business executive. "We were hired on the same day, but in different departments. So long as we were not competing head-to-head, things were fine and we became very close. We had lunch a couple of times a month and spoke on the phone at least once a week. But from the day she was transferred into my work unit, people started telling me that Debbie was bad-mouthing me. One day, when I came back from an off-site meeting, two of my best people reported that Debbie told them that if it wasn't for the fact that they put out great work despite my shortcomings, I'd have been fired a long time ago. I tried to talk things out with Debbie but she denied everything. It's hard to trust behavior like that."

How to stand for something by standing for yourself

By showing disloyalty to a friend and co-worker, Debbie sought to make herself more likeable. Submission—politics—was her way of "purchasing" the approval of others.

The problem, of course, is that by playing politics, the Debbies of this world live unlived lives. By crowding themselves into what they think is another person's image of what is acceptable, they are left with very little real self. No question, the reason they play politics—and this is as true of business and community life as it is of personal and family relationships—is because they believe it to be the way to win personal power. But the irony of it is, submissiveness renders them emotionally invisible. True, they may get their way from time to time. But nobody in their right mind concedes true and abiding power to a ghost.

Personal power at home, on the job, and out in the community demands people who aren't afraid to stand for something, people who decide issues on the basis of what they know, not who they know. You learn to stand for something by standing first for yourself. Self-respect permits us to be a friend to ourself, to recognize that our rights and values need not be sacrificed for the sake of others. Then when we move beyond our personal space into common areas where adaptability is useful, we need to respect others by making decisions and free choices that do not violate the dignity of others.

PRACTICAL PRESCRIPTIONS TO END POLITICAL GAME-PLAYING

My two practical prescriptions are guaranteed to help you feel good about yourself and, at the same time, to act in ways that do not trample on the rights of others.

℞4: Stop inviting disaster.

People who play politics unwittingly set themselves up for disaster. They invite others to ignore their concerns, deny their needs, reject their feelings. Though they rarely come right out and say, "I have no rights, but of course you do. Pardon me for living," that is the effect of their words and gestures. For instance, everyone in a family agrees to participate in yard chores. But when anyone forgets, Dad takes care of it. Within a month, he does all the mowing and raking. Though he is not aware of it, Dad is training the family to ignore his needs. His behavior says, "I don't matter. You can take advantage of me. I'll put up with just about anything to win your admiration."

How to Stop Inviting Failure

1. Be aware of what you say to others and don't use phrases like, "It doesn't really matter to me," and "Do whatever you want. . ."
2. When you speak, make eye contact.
3. Don't shrug your shoulders.

℞5: Start living your own life.

Your chances of awakening the dormant power and confidence within greatly improve when you know what you want and stand up for your rights. Even under normal circumstances, this can be difficult. For the person who has spent a lifetime submitting to others, it can seem insurmountable. I'll have a great deal more to say about exactly how to assert your rights and interests when we get to ℞7. For now, it is enough to be aware that you can change.

Start by thinking of the last time somebody said or did something that made you feel like you wanted to crawl into a shell and let life pass you by. Maybe you were in a crowded movie theatre, so packed you couldn't change seats even though the people behind you were talking. On and on they went, distracting you from the film. You couldn't bring yourself to say anything. So you suffered in silence. And it made you feel worthless. No matter what the particulars of your situation, it probably feels uncomfortable to remember them now. But if you can hold onto the feeling as you read the next couple of pages, I promise to show you a way to take those feelings of discomfort and convert them to a level of personal power such as you may never have felt before. So hang in there.

REPLACE AGGRESSION WITH CHARISMA

Dictators are just as good as everyone else at kidding themselves. They naturally believe there is plenty of reason to think that aggression is the fundamental basis of personal power. But there is even more reason to think it is not.

There is a big difference between the charisma that underlies true personal power and the crude clout that is the foundation of naked aggression. The litmus test is what happens when the dictator is not present. When aggressors relax their iron grip, discipline breaks down in a hurry:

- Children misbehave.
- Employees lose focus.
- Acquaintances drop the ball.

The influence of true personal power, however, abides. People perform as you wish not because you force them to but because they want to. That's why as much happens when the person in possession of true personal power is elsewhere as when he or she is present.

"There's a little bit of the dictator in everybody, but most people are smart enough not to make a habit of acting on it. Sure, I know it's in me and I dislike it," reports Arden Muldoon, an administrator from Salt Lake City. "They say that what we dislike in ourselves is what we dislike most in others. I think that explains why it's so easy for me to hate tyrants."

Six symptoms of aggression and the deadly double bind they produce

In competition for leadership in industry, government, family, and social organizations, aggressive men and women almost always

1. Win arguments
2. Speak loudly
3. Act in ways that are abusive, rude, or sarcastic
4. Dominate subordinates
5. Express feelings, needs, and ideas in ways that tear others down
6. Insist on having the last word

Contrary to appearances, however, their behavior does not come out of supreme confidence in a compelling inner strength. Rather, it arises from a secret fear that they have none and that if they let up they will lose control. This generates the worst sort of double bind: They do not respect the people they dominate (for if they did, they would not violate the dignity of others in the first place), yet they fear a relationship based on equality because it might reveal their own inner weakness.

The late President Richard M. Nixon and his closest advisors often confused aggression with power—Watergate being the best known, but hardly the only, example.

"The thing that is completely misunderstood about Watergate," reports convicted felon and former White House special counsel Charles Colson, "is that everybody thinks the people surrounding the President were drunk with power. But it was insecurity. It began to breed a form of paranoia. We overreacted to the attacks against us. . ."

How to defend your personal perimeter while making a favorable impact on others

Admittedly, some people are aggressive for good causes. Still, they risk paying a high price. The cost is measured in terms of damaged egos and the inability to create and sustain mutually fulfilling social, family, and business relationships.

"When I attended a workshop on handling aggression, they asked us how we coped with dictators," reports Diane Gordimer, a Seattle municipal official. "I made a list of the things people said: Resistance, blaming others, defiance, sabotaging, backstabbing, ganging up, and lying."

Diane's experience delivers a clear and familiar message: Aggression may work for a while, even a long while, but sooner or later the oppressed make their presence felt: Children find ways to reject domineering parents, valued employees vote with their feet.

If aggression is the poison, the antidote is assertiveness. By assertiveness I mean a way of behaving that permits you to feel good about yourself and others, *and* get what you want out of life.

"My students know what I want and that I will stand up for what I believe in," reports Jim Hubschmidt, a Spanish teacher at a Hartford high school. "Because I don't have to act like Hitler to get them to perform, I can use my energy to work with them. That makes me and the kids more comfortable. Does it work? Two of my third-year *estudiantes* took the Spanish S.A.T.s last year. They scored in the top 10 percent."

The assertive person is like the lead guitarist in a rock band: When he isn't taking a solo, he's supporting those who do. People who assert themselves in healthy ways maintain self respect, pursue happiness, satisfy personal needs, and defend personal rights—all without abusing anyone. Just as important, they do not approach others with fears about being hurt or controlled.

THE PRESCRIPTION THAT STOPS AGGRESSION DEAD

Everybody has a personal perimeter that needs to be defended, and we all have the psychological desire to make an impact on the people around us. The following prescription is sure to get others to *want* to give you more of what you want.

℞6: Substitute assertion for aggression.

Earlier, I asked you to recall an incident in which you failed to act in your own behalf. The example I gave was failing to speak up when others in a crowded theatre distracted from your enjoyment of a movie. To show you what I mean when I prescribe assertion, let's carry this example forward.

In every human situation in which somebody violates the rights and space of another, there are basically three action options. You can be submissive, which constrains you to suffer in silence; you can be aggressive and snarl, "Don't you have any respect for others? If you don't shut up this minute, I will call the manager and have you thrown out!" which is likely to provoke a confrontation you cannot win; or you can take the third option, assert your interests, and get what you want.

Asserting your interests in this case takes the form of turning around, looking directly at the talkers, and saying, "When you talk during the picture, it is distracting to me. It makes it hard for me to enjoy the movie."

Assertion offers the best chance of getting what you want. The objective is not to express anger, provoke a confrontation, or belittle anyone else. The whole idea is to change the behavior of others when it intrudes on your life. Ninety-nine times out of a hundred, it is the best way to go.

Let me show you my three-step system for asserting yourself in ways that are useful and constructive. Assume you walk into your workshop at home or on the job only to find several wrenches and a timing meter strewn about. Whoever used them last left the wrenches greasy, the meter cords in a tangle. What's a person to do?

First, you want to describe the offending behavior as specifically as you can without suggesting a motive or character fault, the thing they have done that violates your personal interests:

> "When you don't put my tools away after tuning your car, . . ."

Second, you need to describe how their actions make you feel in ways that are not judgmental, sarcastic, exaggerated, or abusive:

"it makes me feel very upset. . ."

Third, you need to describe, as briefly as you can without harping, the consequences:

"because it means I have to take the time to do it."

Discipline yourself to assert rather than aggress or submit and amazing personal power will enter your life. Not only will you change the behavior of others, you will, at the same time, start building the kinds of relationships that are far stronger and more mutually fulfilling than any you have ever known.

GAIN CREDIBILITY BY CONTROLLING UNMANAGED ANGER

"We lose a surprising number of people because managers don't know how to manage their anger," reports Dick Catcavage, who runs a sports equipment business based in Providence, Rhode Island. "Instead of blowing it off at the appropriate time and being done with it, they let it build up a head of steam. When the pressure gets bad enough, there's no stopping it. The anger trickles out like water through a clenched fist. You see it in all the wrong ways, like snotty remarks or backbiting. People end up making bad decisions simply to get past these problems."

Like my friend Catcavage, I believe there is a place for anger in the normal course of your business, personal, and social relationships. After all, anger is a natural part of the human experience. When it is managed properly—that is, handled in the daily course of events—there is nothing evil or wrong about it. Given legitimate provocation, what is said in the heat of the moment often is intended more to ventilate than to injure. When someone shouts, for instance, the very excitement of the attacker undermines the credibility of his remarks, so they cause little or no permanent pain.

Far more damaging is the unmanaged anger Catcavage talks about. Let me quickly explain: Controlled anger, the good kind of anger, focuses on events—what happened—and has a beginning, a middle, and an end. Unmanaged anger focuses on people—who did it—and produces devastating wounds intended to call a person's self-worth into question.

The dangers of uncontrolled anger

Unmanaged anger is an especially wicked weapon because it diminishes both the perpetrator and the victim and robs them both of personal power. This is truest when the anger comes out in the form of cutting remarks, unfavorable comparisons, needles, teasing, gossip, withdrawal, and the like. Let me give you some quick examples:

Unfavorable comparison "It took me four-and-a-half days to reprogram a sequence in a complicated accounting system," reports Selma Landau, who works in management information systems for a Kansas City greeting card company. "My supervisor looks at the work and says, 'Nick Kountze could've knocked it off in three days.' "

Selma's supervisor hid his anger behind an especially painful mask—the unfavorable comparison. It is a form of attack few people are emotionally secure enough to withstand. We compare ourselves with others to reassure ourselves we are normal, capable, and worthwhile. Being told we are something less than others is a form of anger intended to stir up self-doubt. It has the effect of frightening us.

Belittling Minimizing other people's good points is a second way of disguising anger by belittling people.

"My friend Yolanda wanted to fix me up. So I asked another friend, Marsha, who once dated the man, what he was like," reports Enid Geary, who sings in the chorus of the San Francisco Opera. "Marsha said he was a nice guy when you get to know him. It sounded to me like he was not nice at first. I wondered what he did to her to tick her off."

Teasing, ridicule, and sarcasm A third form of unmanaged anger is teasing, which includes ridicule and sarcasm. Teasing in any form may look like playful humor—it may even have humor in it. Nevertheless, it can be a disguised expression of anger intended to make the person at whom it is directed feel diminished or foolish.

"I'm walking along the MTA platform when this young woman trips and falls. I rush over and ask if she is hurt," reports Evan

Lurtsema, a Boston broker. 'No,' she says, 'I'm down here doing pushups!' By sassing me she didn't do herself any favors. I just walked away without offering to help her get on her feet."

Gossip Gossip is a two-edged thing: it can be a harmless way of venting a little anger or it can be a deliberate way of setting one person against another.

"These two people in my congregation, let's call them Alice and Barbara, were up for the chairmanship of our annual fund-raising dinner dance. They not only knew each other but knew they were in competition. In the course of her interview with the board, Barbara makes a passing remark that Alice is never on time. A few minutes later she says that Alice talks your ear off," reports Dr. Wayne Ortega, a Tampa pastor. "Ordinarily, I would think these remarks weren't very important. But in this case, I got the sense that she was trying to damage Alice's credibility. The board agreed with me on that."

PRACTICAL PRESCRIPTIONS TO STOP UNMANAGED ANGER

If you deny feelings of anger, you are likely to act on them without knowing they are the motivating force behind your responses. This might produce behavior you will later regret. My prescriptions for handling anger will help you bring your feelings out into the open in ways that are both safe and constructive.

℞7: Express anger when it happens and then let it go.

Anger has a beginning, a middle, and an end. Rage has only a beginning and a middle. Because the underlying anger fails to find expression, it does not go away. Every experience of rage is a rehearsal for the next one. The way to prevent rage from taking hold is to deal with anger as it happens, in a constructive way.

In our culture, we are brought up to fear anger in ourselves and others, to feel anxious that it will provoke something dreadful. Husbands and wives are afraid of each other's anger;

employees fear the boss's wrath; salesmen quake when a customer is irritated. We go out of our way to avoid experiencing anger in ourselves or rousing it in others.

The important thing to remember is that anger is natural. When we're denied what we want or get hurt emotionally, we feel anger. Now here's the thing: we can't prevent feeling angry because emotions are not subject to control. But we can control what we do about the feeling. When, as a result of our upbringing, we tell ourselves we'd be better off if we didn't feel angry, we become frightened that something is wrong with us because we cannot prevent it.

Get in the habit of searching out your feelings. Admit them to yourself as much as possible, accept them, express them, and let them go.

℞8: Focus your anger on events, not people.

The best and most useful way to handle your own anger is to focus on what happened, not who did it. The minute you put the onus on the perpetrator, that makes the person fear a counterattack. It sets off a bad chain reaction. The way to prevent it is to take personalities out of the equation. To defuse a situation, show the other person you are not angry with them but with what they did or said.

Prescription Recap

We've covered a lot of ground in this important chapter. Before we move on, it is worth a moment to review my eight practical prescriptions to see if there are any you might have missed.

℞1: Listen better.

℞2: Empathize.

℞3: Find something—anything—useful in what others say.

℞4: Stop inviting disaster by playing politics.

℞5: Start living your own life.

℞6: Substitute assertion for aggression.

℞7: Express anger when it happens and then let it go.

℞8: Focus your anger on events, not people.

Research shows there are four main reasons people don't attain personal power, or achieve less than the full measure of success they desire. Not because they lack intellectual horsepower. Not because they fail to master the skills required for their job. Not because of some technical deficiency. It is because of certain human qualities. It's because of arrogance, political game-playing, aggression, and unmanaged anger.

These have nothing to do with intelligence or experience or education. They have everything to do with character, with human interaction, with the ability to deal with others successfully. When you think about it, that's not so surprising. You see, life is a very human place. It is not theoretical, it's emotional. Dealing with emotions requires sensitivity to others and to yourself.

The positive side to all of this is that, by reading this chapter, you've just bought yourself a ticket. It is your pass to a lifelong journey that should be filled with personal growth, development, and immense satisfaction.

But there is a trick to making the most of this journey. And the four reasons people fail to attain personal power gives you a hint of what it is. If you focus too much on yourself, your needs over the needs of others, you are likely to run into a lot of issues that are sure to cut your trip short. But if you focus instead on the people in your life, your journey will be a long and rewarding one—and personal power and confidence are certain to be yours.

In the chapters ahead, I am going to develop the idea of focusing on people within the framework of two big concepts: first, that the key to personal power and confidence is to condition your mind to deal successfully with others; and second, what it takes to feel and act powerful and confident.

Eleven Ways to Take Control of Your Business and Personal Relationships

"You are looking at the one guy in the crowd people always forgot to introduce," reports Vincent Von Ancken, a Sacramento collectibles dealer. "I'll never forget the day I couldn't take it anymore. I looked myself in the eye. The face in the bathroom mirror wasn't me. It was the face of a 97-pound weakling who is always being bullied.

"I never felt like I enjoyed life the ways it's meant to be lived. I felt like a lightweight when it came to other people. What I had to say or think or do wasn't as important to me as what other people wanted to talk about. I used to blame everybody else for dissing me, dismissing me, dumping all over me. But you know, when I looked into that mirror I somehow finally saw that I didn't respect myself; I was doing the dissing, dismissing, and dumping . . . on myself! That's when I found a way to tap into the inner power that's making my dreams come true. Now, people want to see things my way. Whether it is surrounding myself with a close circle of friends and family, or a room full of strangers, I know how to get what I need, when I want it, without a lot of hassle."

Let's be honest: everybody craves what personal power begets. Business people want orders. Politicians want votes. Labor wants wages. Bosses want loyalty. Colleagues want recognition. Friends want trust. Lovers want valentines. Parents want obedience. Children want security. Everybody wants respect.

How to Awaken the Power Within

Like my friend Vincent, you too may find yourself part of the pardon-me-for-living crowd. You go through life making a human doormat out of yourself to get what you need. In your heart of hearts you know servility is a hit-or-miss proposition, but that doesn't stop you. Failure after failure hasn't made your life as rewarding and as full as it is for other people, yet you continue to repeat the heartbreaking pattern. How to explain it?

You probably tell yourself it's because your genetic code somehow lacks the gene for the traction it takes to get people to *want* to be part of whatever it is you have in mind. But as you will quickly discover, every normal human being is born with exactly the raw ingredients it takes to make his and her every dream come true. All you've got to do is use them. Therein lies the catch. No one's ever shown you how to leverage what is as much a part of your God-given birthright as anybody else's.

That's why I feel confident that, for you, this chapter is sure to be the red alert you need to open new vistas of business and social success. Here in these pages, I am going to show you eleven dependable ways to kickstart the awesome but dormant power within—how to turn your life around at home, on the job, and out in the community in ways that, for the moment, you can only dream about. When I say turn your life around, I am not talking about in a year, a month, or even a week. I am talking about making your life different and better by the time you finish this chapter.

Each of my eleven practical prescriptions is a proven and workable way to command personal power in any and every area of living—in relationships, among the people you work with and for, even in community and social settings. Make these prescriptions part of your daily living and you cannot fail to experience the thrill of walking into rooms full of new faces knowing you've got what it takes to make things happen. Rehearse them, apply them every chance you get and these two amazing benefits are yours when you command personal power in every area of life:

1. In no time at all people who once ignored you, even strangers of the opposite sex, will be held spellbound by your views and ideas.
2. On the job, men and women who once might have dismissed you will suddenly and gladly give you their full and unqualified support.

THE MEANING OF PERSONAL POWER

Before we get to my eleven practical prescriptions, let's take a minute to agree on what we mean when we talk about personal power.

Some people take as gospel the idea that power is clout. It's an immaculate misconception. The way I see it, personal power has nothing to do with force, threats, or intimidation. Instead, it's about the ability to satisfy the craving that exists within each and every human being for affirmation.

Let me explain. Our feelings about ourselves are, to some extent, reflections of the feelings other people have, or seem to have, about us. We need other people to help us feel important, confirm our sense of worth. They need as much from us.

Ego hunger, the need for affirmation, is as natural, universal, and important as the hunger for food. The body needs calories, the ego needs what can come only from others:

1. Acceptance
2. Approval
3. Appreciation

HOW TO MAKE OTHERS WANT TO BE WITH YOU

If you conclude that relationships drive power, you are at least half right. You also need to recognize that what we are dealing with is not just a matter of quantity but also of quality. The better you make each relationship, the more personal power you accrue.

I want to expand on this last thought by pointing out that the people who loom largest in our lives—wives, husbands, leaders, lovers, teachers, professionals, bosses, parents, children—are the ones whose good opinion of us is worth more even than our own. So long as they nourish our self-esteem they can injure us, steal our goods, damage us in all kinds of ways and still get by. After all, when they feed our ego we are more confident, cheerful, generous, tolerant, and willing to listen. That makes it easy and natural to be spiritually generous. We think of their needs and the way we can repay their interest and satisfy them. We are, in other words, in their power.

The more power you give, the more power you get

All human dealings, whatever else they may appear to be, are based on fulfilling (or failing to fulfill) these needs. Unless you live in total isolation, you exercise power over others all of the time. Whether you connect or miss, speak or stand silent, act or remain passive, everything you say (or fail to say) affects, to some degree, other people's views of themselves. The more you satisfy their hunger for respect, recognition, and acceptance, the more they want to be with you. The more they want to be with you, the more power you develop. Let me illustrate the point with a quick example.

The Rev. Dr. Martin Luther King, Jr. told of two prominent civil rights leaders who flew into Atlanta to confer with him. Before talks began, an airport porter sweeping the floor drew Dr. King aside.

After 15 minutes, one of the leaders was heard to grumble bitterly, "I haven't come a thousand miles to sit and wait while he talks to a common porter."

"When the day comes that he does not use his power to recognize the needs of a common porter," the other replied, "on that day I will not have time to come even one mile to see him."

Dr. King's experience illustrates that his power arose not only (or, even, mostly) from the way he viewed himself. It came from the way he was viewed by others.

What is true of Dr. King is as true of you, me, and the man in the moon. We are powerful to the degree we establish and maintain good relationships with others—influence the positive ways in which others see us. Remember, whether we are porters or princes, our wellsprings of personal power are all one and the same: the people with whom we interact. Among them, we gain when we give.

Try as we may to be our own emotional 911, nothing erases the heartache of knowing we need and deserve, but fail to win, the affirmation we crave.

Practical Prescriptions for Taking Control of Relationships

The fact you are reading this chapter says you recognize the need for things to change. After all, you cannot possibly become what you hope to be by remaining what you are.

℞1: Look yourself in the eye.

The question, "Where to begin?" is best answered with honest self-acceptance. I am talking about realizing that your problem doesn't reside elsewhere. It's part of you because you are all of it. Don't be too surprised to discover that this is good news. You see, if the source of your power problems is others, you are stuck. There is nothing you can do to change them. This way, you at least have a shot at getting yourself on the right course.

The following exercise will help you see yourself in more realistic terms. It's based on the idea of the personals in magazines or newspapers—the columns where people advertise themselves.

If you had to write a personal ad describing the kind of person you are, you might want it to sound something like this:

Available: Attractive, sensitive, honest, healthy, faithful, respectful person who is successful but not a workaholic, adventurous but intimate, strong but tender, energetic yet warm. Appreciates, accepts, and approves of others, good sense of humor, ready to share.

Here's the exercise. Tape a blank piece of paper to your bathroom mirror. Each morning for a week, I want you to take a long, hard look at yourself in the mirror. Then I want you to write down the most negative quality you see. Don't write a whole sentence. Just sum up what you see in a word or two; for example, *unaccepting.* At the end of the week, read over the list of the negative qualities. Here's an example of what such a list might look like:

Angry
Loser
Complainer
In a dead-end job
Moody
Spineless
Hard to get along with

Now that you've noted some of your most unattractive qualities, it's time to write a want ad based on your list. Make the ad as direct as you can. The more outrageous you make the ad sound, the more it can help you to see yourself as others might.

> **Available:** Do you hate yourself? Do you hate the world? Angry loser long on potential but doing nothing seeks person who values empty promises and likes taking the blame for everything that goes wrong.

Obviously, none of us would ever write an ad like this but, by forcing you to take a look at how you see yourself—by taking what has been unconscious and making it apparent—writing your own ad is a powerful way to break your own negative programming.

Recognizing yourself is the beginning of success. Before you can attract power you've got to understand what you are doing and how to either correct it or work around it.

HOW YOU MAY BE ROBBING YOURSELF OF POWER

Let me repeat what I said in the first chapter. Only when you recognize and understand that the impact of your behavior causes people to respond to you in ways that rob you of confidence and undermine power can you hope to find a way around your mistakes.

Ask yourself the following questions to make the look inward more informed:

- Do I have a short fuse?
- Do I respond with tears?
- Do I lie?
- Do I tell the truth when it only serves to hurt others?
- Do I worry excessively?
- Am I always asking the advice of others before making a decision?
- Do I have difficulty owning up to a mistake?

If you answer yes to one or more of these questions, please read on. In the pages ahead you'll find the solutions you need to make your future more confident and secure.

Many, many people have the deep feeling that, because they are without power, they are somehow unworthy. These people defend against this unpleasant feeling by imprisoning themselves in a certain image or lifestyle. Whether they come on bashful or belligerent, it's all a cover-up. To get rid of the mask, all they've got to do is look themselves in the eye.

℞2: Accept that power is within your power.

It is always within your power to add to the feeling of personal worth people crave. It is within your power to make them feel better about themselves. It is within your power to confirm their importance both to themselves and to you. It adds up to a wealth of power. The great tragedy is that so many of us either hoard this wealth or never recognize we possess it.

"Give it away indiscriminately; in so doing you need not worry about getting what you want from others," reports author Les Giblin. "When you cast this bread upon the waters, so to speak, it always comes back to you multiplied many fold."

The following exercise will help you see just how much power you possess:

On two sheets of paper, write: *It is within my power.* Tape one to the top of your desk. Tape the other to your bathroom mirror. For a week, every time you see one of these notes, try to experience what it might feel like to make somebody, anybody, feel good about themselves. At the end of seven days a subtle but amazing change will have taken place. Suddenly you will be much more comfortable with the power that comes with your birth certificate. Keep it up for another week or two and your comfort index is certain to rise even higher.

℞3: Look for the win-win option.

A win-lose approach to power—If-I-get-it-you-lose-it—is like a stopped clock. Twice a day it looks right, but it really never is. And if you don't see things quite that way, you are in for a very disappointing reading experience. You won't find a line in this book intended to help you make a victim of yourself. Let me put it to you as straight as I can: The more it seems to work, the more a win-lose strategy defeats you in the end. Here's why:

Only a satisfied ego can afford to be generous with others. Each time you inflict a loss on another person you choke off a little more of the nourishment their ego craves. A famished ego is so worried about further erosion of self-esteem, it sets up an invisible shield. Very little gets in; even less gets out. Bye-bye power.

"For years people have been coming to me wondering if there's some kind of magic elixir that makes people better leaders. I always tell them yes, there is," reports Milwaukee management training consultant Mary Francis Baltzer. "All you have to remember is that a win-lose setup drives people whereas win-win propositions make them *want* to follow your lead."

The moment you give other people good reason to think well of themselves, you take instant control of the business and personal relationships that shape your life, your dreams, your destiny. Since you possess and need what others require and offer, it is clearly in your interest to follow Baltzer's lead: Give people the satisfied egos they want and you are guaranteed the personal power you crave.

"I recall one time when a young man in my brand group wrote a two-page memorandum proposing our company go into a new business," reports Procter & Gamble CEO Edwin Artzt. "It was approved. A day later, Neil McElroy, the Chairman, shows up in my doorway. He wonders if this young man really is all that he appears to be. I say he is. 'Well then,' says McElroy, 'let's promote him.' We did. I must say the young man's attitude and work ethic made us all feel like winners that day, believe me."

Artzt is telling you the best business reason in the world to make the win-win option your number one priority: It pays.

℞4: Listen.

If you think powerful people know something you don't, you're right. They know how to listen.

I am sure you have noticed that some of the most powerful people in your life have a knack for tuning into what others say. They may not always agree with you but you can bet the farm that what you just said is what they just heard.

Whether your goal is a corner office, a better marriage, or a greater feeling of satisfaction in life, listening does more to create win-win situations than anything else you can name. Most people are dying to tell you what they need. All you've got to do is listen. Knowing their desires helps you figure out their side of the equation—what you can offer that will make them feel good about themselves.

> By "listen," I mean concentrate on everything the other person has to say. Of course, everything they say won't aid your cause, but some of it will. Train yourself to listen with all you've got. Among the responses are sure to be many, if not all, of the ones you need.
>
> "I had a bad strep throat the night of my fourth date with Margo. It hurt to talk. So I just listened. Funny thing, I learned more about her that night than I had in the first three dates combined," reports Will Diefenderfer, who works in resource management for the State of Alaska. "By listening as long and strong as she wanted, I caught on to what she needed to feel okay with herself and with me."

Better listening serves two purposes: First, it enables you to capture the critical content of what is being said; second, it leads others to see you as a person who grasps what is said.

Four ways to listen better

1. When the conversation is face-to-face, make eye contact and hold it 60 to 70 percent of the time. On the phone, send an occasional "verbal nod" to your partner: "Yes. . . ," "I see. . . .," "Um . . ."
2. Lean towards the other person with an expression of friendly concentration on your face. Try not to fidget.
3. Don't interrupt or jump to conclusions. Allow them to speak their piece fully and freely.
4. Resist asking too many questions by putting more effort into listening than trying to figure out ways to argue against what the other person is saying.

Remember, others can hardly wait to tell you everything you need to know to make them feel good about themselves. All you've got to do is listen like you mean it.

℞5: Ask open-ended questions.

Open-ended questions help you explore the other person's mindset—what they need from you to feel good about themselves.

What's the difference between an open-ended and a limiting question? An open-ended question cannot be answered by yes, no, or with a fact. It is an invitation. It invites the other person to talk more or less freely about the way they see and experience things. Let me show you what I mean:

"A ballerina. You're kidding! Really?! Are you really a ballerina?" is an example of a limiting question. The answer is either yes or no. Either way, it amounts to a response in search of a better question. You don't want to know if she is a ballerina. You need to find her hot button. Limited questions produce limited information. Unless you strike it lucky, these questions are unlikely to give you a line on what it will take from you to make her feel good about herself.

Here's the same idea in open-ended form: "A ballerina. You're kidding. Really?! What does it feel like to be a ballerina?"

Her response is certain to give you a clue to what she needs. For instance, suppose she says, "It's the thrill of a lifetime to dance for an enthusiastic audience."

You might conclude that being a ballerina appeals to her desire to find recognition. That's enough to build a win-win option that bridges the gap between your interests and hers.

"I know that, being a ballerina and all, you're always before the public. But what the Cancer Society is asking you to do is make an appearance with a special part of the public. I am talking about kids with cancer. We think they'll give you the kind of grateful recognition you can't find anywhere else but on the face of a sick kid."

Five ways to ask open-ended questions

Generally speaking, open-ended questions begin with the letter *W*. The possibilities are limitless. Here are five for starters:

1. Who are your heroes?
2. What's the real story on this deal?
3. Where would you live if you could live anywhere in the world?
4. When you say that, are you thinking about something specific?
5. Why do you suppose Riley put Starks back in the game?

℞6: Admit that other people are important.

Give yourself 10 seconds to take this little two-part exercise:

1. Think of what you might accomplish as the only person on earth.
2. Now think of how much more you might accomplish as one among billions.

I know the point sounds basic, but you've got to believe me: People are important. You can't have, get, or hold power all by your lonesome. Power is all about how other people see you. You want power? You need people!

Admit that people are important and a whole new attitude comes over you. It shows up in the more welcoming way you offer a friend a handshake, the more confident way you enter and move through a crowd of people. Other people admire that sort of thing, want to be like that, and want to be next to people who are like that. Net, net, people who believe other people are important have the power to influence us.

"Here's the number-one rule I followed to develop my leadership," wrote industrialist Henry J. Kaiser. He built the San Francisco Bay Bridge and Hoover Dam, and owned steel mills, car factories, and shipyards. "I try to recognize that if the other guy is an SOB he's still a child of God . . . and that makes him an important SOB."

℞7: Pay attention to others.

With our sound-bite culture and fast-food mentality, it's a hurry-up world we inhabit. There's hardly time to see what's what, never mind smell the roses. So when others take a moment to notice us, they are giving us a pretty big compliment. They recognize our importance.

"In dollars and cents, it definitely pays to pay attention to your people," reports Jay Philpott, a University of Michigan statistician. "The data from annual studies going all the way back to 1949 are consistent. They tell us supervisors interested in the people working for them get more performance than the bossy type who pull an attitude that says managers know it all and peons have to do it all."

℞8: Make more of others to make more of yourself.

You, me, everybody—we're all subject to a basic fact of human nature: We all need to feel important and to feel that other people recognize our importance. This means that when we deal with others, the temptation is always present to impress them. Resist it.

"I make good impressions for a living," reports Chicago sales consultant Jean Cuzak. "The best way I ever found for impressing people is to let them know that I am impressed by them. Giving them importance by noticing things like their skills, or track record of success, or spirit doesn't take anything away from me. It just shows them I respect who they are and what they are accomplishing."

If we had any, a lot of us would like to believe our own press clippings. Which means, of course, that a lot of us are probably acting in ways designed to impress others with our own importance. If someone tells a good story, we try to top it. One result of doing so is to make them feel small. Somehow, this is supposed to make us feel more important—but I don't get it. Here's the way I see it: What really happens is that we give off egotistical vibes. So the more we puff ourselves up, the lonelier we are apt to become. On the other hand, give others reason to believe you are impressed by them and their esteem for you cannot fail to grow.

"I said to her father first time I met him that anybody who could raise as fine a daughter as Dorothy certainly knows something worth learning," reports Jim Bastis, who lives and works in Portland, Oregon. "That got me a real firm handshake at first, and a lot of fine bass fishing trips together ever since."

Jim's experience reaffirms my point: making more of them makes more of you.

℞9: Practice acceptance.

Acceptance is shorthand for allowing others to be themselves while you remain you. You don't have to like them, don't have to agree with anything. All you have to do is not force them to live up to your idea about how people are supposed to be.

"We all get one life and plenty of opportunity to screw it up," reports John Lloyd-Owen, a transportation manager from Indianapolis. "Even if you think someone's doing something stupid, you have to accept their basic right to be wrong."

Do you want people to grant you the power you seek? Then remember one of the most fundamental laws of human nature: What goes around comes around. Adopt the attitude of acceptance you want others to express and you'll get as much in return.

"If you've ever walked out of a store without buying something because the clerk turned you off, you know what I am talking about," reports Oklahoma City retail sales manager Jeff Coulter. "If the attitude you project doesn't make the sale, it is going to break it."

HOW TO BE MORE ACCEPTING OF OTHERS

Acceptance—the ability to separate people from their behavior—reflects a view of life in which right and wrong are largely irrelevant.

- Pay no attention to what people are not. Begin immediately to accept others for who and what they are. Fake it if you must. As you begin to see acceptance work *for* instead of *against* your interests, your heart will follow.

- Stop insisting that people have to be perfect before you even allow them to approach.
- Don't impose rigid standards that others have to meet before you accept them.

℞10: Practice approval.

Accepting someone means allowing them to be themselves; approval means finding something—even the tiniest of details—you can think well of.

"I run a division of about 3,000 people worldwide. I don't know them all but I'd probably like a lot of them. But like them or not, I've got budgets to meet so I've got to get each of them to perform as though I do," reports Chantal Paradiso, an agribusiness manager in California's Central Valley. "The trick is to remember that each of them does something good. Even if it's only a little thing, it keeps personal feelings from getting in the way."

Despite your overall feelings, there is at least one thing about anybody—even your worst enemy—you can approve of. If you don't believe me, just take a moment to think about your worst enemy. Now think of something—anything—you can approve. The color of his socks. The way she follows through on a golf swing. Since no one is 100 percent anything, even in the darkest picture you paint there must be—has to be—at least one positive thing. Find it. When you do, and let the other person experience your approval, they will go out of their way to give you the power you desire and deserve.

℞11: Practice appreciation.

One of the most important things we seek from others is a sense of being valued. That's what appreciation is all about. When they appreciate you, they are saying you are important. In doing so, they raise your value.

SIX WAYS TO SHOW OTHERS YOU APPRECIATE THEM

It can be as simple as treating other people's time as valuable as yours and never keeping them waiting, if you can help it. Finding something to appreciate in the other person gives them reason to feel good about themselves—which normally leads to them feeling good about you.

1. Use their names in the course of conversation, but don't overdo it.
2. Don't lump people by age, occupation, or geography. Treat them as individuals and not as old-timers or teenagers; as people and not as machinists or lawyers; as neighbors and not as southerners or Yankees.
3. In a business or social setting, take notice of the leaders, but also pay attention to the rest of the crowd.
4. Treat men and women as equals. Direct your attention to both.
5. Don't be put off when people act up. It might be their way of telling you they are not getting the attention they want.
6. Pay attention to little things. Notice a new hairdo. Remember birthdays or other special occasions.

All of these tell people you consider them important enough to pay special attention to the things that ring their bells.

PRESCRIPTION RECAP

To be sure you've gotten the main points of my eleven practical prescriptions, let me quickly recap them for you.

℞ 1: Look yourself in the eye.

℞ 2: Accept that power is within your power.

℞ 3: Look for the win-win option.

℞ 4: Listen.

℞ 5: Ask open-ended questions.

℞ 6: Admit that other people are important.

℞ 7: Pay attention to others.

℞ 8: Make more of others to make more of yourself.

℞ 9: Practice acceptance.

℞10: Practice approval.

℞11: Practice appreciation.

The more you understand power, the more power you have. I think by now the point has been made. There is a big difference between somebody doing what you want because they want to and doing it because they feel pressured into it. Pressure tactics may work once in a while, perhaps even for limited periods. But the moment you take your finger off the trigger, you render yourself a weakling . . . again.

On the other hand, true personal power is a wonderfully self-fulfilling prophecy. The more ways you show people you understand what power is all about, the more power they're going to give you.

By freely giving others the very things you want yourself—acceptance, approval, and appreciation—you take control of your life in a way that is more productive than anything else you have ever known before.

In the next chapter, I am going to show you how to take this solid foundation for personal growth that is now yours and leverage it. Because you never get a second chance to make a good first impression, I want you to know from the get-go how to make the impression you make on others the right one.

Seven Ways to Make a Lasting Impression and Increase Your Value and Importance to Others

". . . so I said, 'Gee, Lin, come on. We've walked a pretty long road together...,'" reports Ross Brisker, a native of Washington's Yakima Valley.

"I made a little joke on the phone. It wasn't out of line. But, you know, with Linda's mother dying out in Boise and she being so hyper and all, well, she took it wrong. Accused me of attacking her. Me? Well now, don't that beat all. Anybody else said it, I'd've been ticked off for sure. But here's this woman made my life a whole lot richer for knowing her. She's in a hard place. Well, I love her, and that's a fact. I mean, I wasn't feeling too much love at that minute. But I could remember a whole bunch of it—all the way back to meeting her on a rafting trip on the Salmon. So, hey, yeah, the old warm-and-fuzzies helped us get through it okay."

The moral of the story? Thank goodness first takes are unforgettable! Years after Ross and Linda first ran into each other, the favorable but subconscious memories—the "warm-and-fuzzies"—of their earliest encounter go to work in his mind. The unseen but powerful emotional lift of these impressions tide him over temporarily rough waters. Ross may or may not remember the words they first spoke. But he's never forgotten the first impression she made on him.

That the impressions we make—first as well as subsequent—have a life beyond the moment in which we create them may sound like a complication we could live easily without. Actually, it simplifies things. I say that because all you've got to do to make your dreams come true is make sure the impression you leave of yourself is always the right one. I know my words sound like a platitude, but they're not. They're more than the best way to steadily increase your value and importance among others: They are the only way. As best you can, you must start from, build on, and build with positive impressions if you are out to steadily increase your value and importance to others. The only question is, How?

What It Takes to Make the Right Impression

To tell you what it takes to make the right impression, I've got two choices: I can refer you to libraries filled with books on the topic or I can save you a lot of time by saying that they all deliver the same basic message. Let me sum up their combined wisdom for you in just three letters: *Y-O-U*.

The world forms its opinion of you mainly from the opinion you have of yourself. This, too, is based on a law of psychology that is as certain as sunrise: Whenever you encounter people, what you say and what you don't say, how you look and how you don't look set the stage for everything that follows.

If you think of yourself as shy, fearful, a nobody, that's the impression you will create. Think like a winner and people will happily recognize the positive side of your personality.

A Practical Program to Put You in Control of the Impressions You Make

In these pages you will find proven and workable techniques certain to help you make the kinds of impressions that get you more of what you want out of life. In daily use for over 25 years, these have been tested, debugged, and refined by thousands of rising managers at some of America's most successful corporate giants. The growing livelihoods of these men and women, from many walks of life, hinge on creating an atmosphere of success among colleagues, customers, and the community at large. If my methods work for them under highly competitive business conditions, they are certain to do as much for you at home, on the job, and socially. In fact, I guarantee it. Faithfully applied, the techniques that give some of the country's top managers a leg-up against competition cannot fail to help you establish the base of personal power and respect human leadership demands.

Before this chapter ends, you are going to have seven practical ways to steadily improve your value and importance to others. Amplified with honest-to-life examples you can follow and be guided by, these show you, step-by-step:

- Tested ways to impress people favorably simply by being yourself—even if you are quiet, unassertive, or simply not the congenial person you'd like to be.
- Proven ways to relate better, improve your life, and still be yourself—all without manipulating anyone in any way.

Make these practical prescriptions part of your everyday life, practice them every chance you get, systematically build them up, and two marvelous benefits will be yours forever:

1. Suddenly and instantly you will reach a new and attractive level of personal power. Whether you're asking for an order, a raise, or a first date, you are certain to open the hearts, minds, and pocketbooks of people at home, on the job, and in the community.
2. The balance of power will shift in your favor as you work to establish your new, more purposeful, but wholly authentic personality. Control of your life will move from forces outside of yourself to the inner power and confidence that is your birthright.

HOW TO WIN FRIENDS FOR LIFE IN TEN SECONDS OR LESS

I'd like you to start benefiting from my practical prescriptions just as quickly as good sense allows. But first, we ought to agree on four basic principles.

1. *Only hermits can afford to ignore the impressions they make.* After all, they never see anyone twice. But you do.

   It's a well-proven fact that the success you enjoy in your career has less to do with your job skills than with the impressions you make on your customers and colleagues. Your each and every personal friendship begins with two sets of impressions. Yours. And theirs. This also explains the obverse: you never get to first-base with that certain stranger because your first impression strikes out. The roles that blossom for you in church and community affairs all sprout from the imprint you plant in the minds of people you respect.

2. *Impressions are made before we know it.* As we meet people, a hidden process takes place in our minds. We form instant but, for the most part, unspoken opinions about the kinds of human beings they are, the values they hold, the goals that drive them, and so on. So deeply are these buried, we may not be conscious of them.

   "I never did put my finger on what made me decide not to offer Herb Semmel a partnership," reports lawyer Althea Rathburn, of San Antonio. "He did a good job for his clients. But, well, every time I thought about doing it, something in me said it's not such a good idea."

   It's a safe guess that hardly a day goes by you don't hear someone say he or she doesn't know why they don't like so-and-so or this-and-that. "It's, you know, just a feeling." Well, like Althea's, that feeling says a lot and implies even more. It says, once upon a time a kernel of distrust—which Althea associates with Herb—was sown in her mind. And it implies it is down so deep in her emotions it doesn't even have a name. No wonder words can't get it out.

3. *Unexpressed emotions create psychological tension.* Tension demands relief. We release it in the only way we can. We call

it *feelings*. Vague though it may be, it was such a feeling that cost Herb Semmel a promotion. It seems to me rather a high price to have to pay for a poor impression. Yet there it is.

4. *Assessments are made and cast in concrete instantaneously*. These mental snapshots condition our feelings about, and behavior toward, somebody. In our minds they are and will largely remain what they first appear to us . . . even if, at any point in time, we can't say flat-out what it is.

   - Come across cross and, even though you're basically a Mother Teresa type, it'll do you no good. He'll always harbor the shred of a nagging feeling. Deep down, he wonders if maybe you are something of a closet kvetch.
   - Make a better imprint, one that leads her to imagine a halo over your head and a wonderful thing will happen . . . and happen . . . and keep on happening. From that moment on, even when the going gets rough, part of her will secretly be driven by the emotional memory of what a truly sincere and spiritually generous person you are.

You Never Get a Second Chance to Make a First Impression

Because the essence of the impressions you create secretly endure, you must go all-out to establish solid footings from the get-go. When you project a more confident attitude, the power to make things happen—to take control of your life—is yours.

Act with confidence and others are more likely to have confidence in you; act powerless and the response that greets you is likely to be the moral equivalent of a pie in the puss.

℞1: Don't be what you are not.

Not only do I think you are a hundred percent capable of truly becoming the person you want others to see, I am certain of it. I say this because, in my experience, people who see themselves lacking power and confidence subconsciously communicate more about their weaknesses than their strengths. Strangers pick up on these negative vibes and judge accordingly. The shame of it is, they never get to see any (or enough) of the positives.

The mere fact that you are reading this book tells me that, if you are at all normal, buried somewhere in your personal geology lies a seam of 24-karat gold. The gold mine is there no matter who you are and how little you think of yourself. And it's everything you need to awaken the power and confidence within, turn your life around, win the regard and respect you crave. The treasure I am talking about is the person you'd be if you were totally at peace with yourself.

Job one is to find and liberate the positive side of the inner you. Yes, the work of it is to change the signals you send to others. This is not the same as having to create a new you out of thin air. No, what I want you to do is become more fully yourself. Accentuate the positive instead of the negative.

I know the process of self-emergence seems as risky as yanking on a sweater's yarn. The fear of unravelling yourself completely is there. But, believe me, once you make the decision to become all you are, you'll wonder what took you so long.

If there is some easier way to become more completely yourself I'd like to be the first one to tell you about it. But there isn't. There's no other way. You cannot possibly hope to be seen in new ways by remaining what you are.

HOW TO FIND AND MAKE THE MOST OF YOUR HIDDEN ASSETS

The whole idea is to look into yourself: to see, perhaps for the first time, your hidden strengths as well as the weaknesses that stare you in the face; to experience in a new way things about yourself you probably take for granted, hidden assets you fail to exploit. I'm talking about sifting through your values, beliefs, and behaviors to find things about yourself that you respect and that other people might find attractive.

Here are a few examples of the personal assets people are finding these days:

- A fortyish woman reports she is surprised to discover one of her hidden strengths is the "sort of decency that gets you to make those tough phone calls and visits when a friend's parent lies dying."
- A manager up in Portland, Maine writes, "Self-examination gets me to realize I want to be able to work with and through others, even though I come on like a loner."
- At a family dinner, a friend's pre-teen niece—a shy person by nature—takes a look inside and concludes, "My best thing is that I am very good with cats and dogs."

Here's the catch: No matter who you are, there's just one way to access the buried El Dorado within. You can't fake it, make a snow job, pretend. You can't get somebody to do it instead of you. No shortcut will do. You've got to dig your way to pay dirt. It's as the famous sculptor says: the finished statue is already in the stone. The artist does not create it so much as liberate it.

Hard work? Not with the system I am going to lay out for you in the next practical prescription. No matter, though. Easy or hard, one thing is for sure: The rewards justify the effort.

"Not in my wildest dreams could I imagine a time when I could succeed by being myself," reports Orlando's Margot Bunten, an assistant TV producer. "I used to not like myself a lot. There are parts of me I still don't really cotton to. But I've discovered other things about me that really are different, that I respect in myself in a way that gets other people to respect me back. Now, it's a relief not manipulating people into thinking I am something I am not and then having to struggle against the tide to try and live up to it, when what I am is perfectly good enough."

Mind Margot's words well. They illustrate the importance of personal authenticity. Life is better and more rewarding for all concerned when you are more fully the person you really are as opposed to fooling people into seeing you as someone you are not.

Searching within, envisioning yourself in new ways—these empower you to leverage your strengths against the opportunities life affords. Think of the decision to become yourself as the first step in making your dreams come true. It's dreaming the dream, and that's very important. You can't make a dream come true if you don't dream the dream in the first place.

"Show me a stock clerk with an honest vision of himself," wrote James Cash Penney, founder of the well-known mercantile chain, "and I will show you a person capable of making history. On the other hand, show me someone capable of making history but without an inner vision and I will show you a stock clerk."

℞2: Identify and release the real you.

To help you locate and liberate the personal assets that will surely enlarge your life and attract others, I have prepared an exercise that's both painless and revealing.

The following chart is divided into two sections, Weakness and Strength. Beneath these are five ruled lines. This is where you come in. In the appropriate spaces, I want you to list your five greatest weaknesses and strengths. The catch is, you may not put down a weakness without at the same time putting down something about yourself you respect. That's all there is to it: For every weakness you must write down a strength. We'll discuss the implications as soon as you are done.

Weakness	Strength

The point of the exercise is to show you that whether you choose to use them or not, you possess hidden strengths as well as more self-evident weaknesses.

In my third practical prescription, I'll show you how to use the strengths you have just brought to the surface to attract new friends and influence people. Meanwhile, if you decide in the future to repeat this exercise, do not be surprised to see yourself making different notations. It is perfectly normal to experience yourself in different ways over time and in the light of events.

℞3: Speak of who you are in terms of what they want.

It is a well-established fact that people listen to themselves more than they listen to you or anybody else. This is so because everybody acts out of self-interest. It's an idea as old as the Bible. Remember the lesson of Babel: When what you say does not relate to people, people will not relate to what you say.

We filter the world through our needs. So it figures: If you will simply identify and present your strengths in terms of what others need—come at things from their angle as well as your own—they cannot fail to see you as you wish to be seen.

THE TEN BASICS EVERYONE NEEDS

Psychologists tell us ten basic drives are at work in everybody all of the time. They say the need for power and the need to feel important are the most motivating. That means you can almost always slant your strengths in ways that appeal to a person's need to feel superior. But there is often more to human need than power and control. Here are ten needs that, alone or in combination, motivate people:

1. *Affection*—a yearning to belong
2. *Ego*—a sense of personal pride
3. *Esteem*—a passion to be admired by others
4. *Excellence*—a need to win
5. *Greed*—a need for more than a fair share
6. *Liberty*—an urge to control personal destiny
7. *Power*—a need for superiority
8. *Privacy*—a desire to protect personal space

9. *Recognition*—a need for personal worth
10. *Security*—a need for protection from threat

When you understand the secret needs that drive other people to think as they do, you can easily establish yourself in positive terms. All you've got to do is look at your strengths through the lens of their needs. Then, based on what you see, present the authentic you in terms they want to hear. This makes it extremely easy for them to see you in the positive way you wish to be seen.

"Nellie Forbush has got to be the best salesperson in the business," reports Je Woo Yeom, from Norfolk. "We're in a roller-coaster industry so we need reliable vendors—people with a strong stick-to-it attitude. First time she calls on me she tells me 90 percent of her sales are to accounts she's called on for two or more years. I'm so impressed I give her an opening order on the spot. That's four years ago. Today she's one of our fifty top sources."

Self-Test: How to Be the Person You Dream of Becoming

The point of this exercise is to show you how easy it is to apply your new-found assets to increase your value and importance to others.

To proceed, you'll need a list of your five greatest personal strengths. With this in hand, I want you to read the ten situations I've sketched below.

In each situation, imagine yourself in the encounter. At the end of each scenario, you will be asked to mentally note two things: first, the other person's need, as you perceive it; and second, how one or more of your strengths relate to their need. Here's a quick example of what I am talking about:

> *You are called in for a job interview with architect Clifton Wegner. Wegner, whose trailblazing work regularly appears in national magazines and TV, wants to hire an office manager. As you enter, he rummages through his desk. "I can remember the details of buildings from 20 years ago," he says, "but I can't for the life of me remember what I just did with my keys."*

You conclude that, though Cliff is up to his eyeballs in creativity, he is like a helium-filled balloon. He needs to have a string attached so that he can be prevented from flying away entirely. You would enjoy being that string.

Among the inner strengths you possess and, during the course of the interview, relate to Cliff's need for solid, businesslike support, you identify:

1. *Patience ("It gives me a good feeling to finish a project two years in the making.")*
2. *An eye for detail ("Are these your keys?")*
3. *The ability to take care of others—ministering, nursing, helping sorts of activities ("I may be the only person you'll ever meet who enjoys writing progress reports for the office.")*

As you proceed with this exercise, remember that there are no right or wrong answers, no time limit. Simply read each encounter and mentally note the needs you pick up on, and how you'd match one or more of your strengths against them. That's all there is to it. We'll discuss the implications of your answers when you have completed this exercise.

1. *At a family wedding reception, you spot the dazzling Joanne Berghold. The tall, lissome, blonde makes friendly eye contact. Though you feel uncertain about talking with someone as good looking as she, the idea intrigues you. As you approach to strike up a conversation, you overhear her say to the person beside her, "I think it's worse to be in a rut than to have your head in the clouds."*
   A. Identify the principal need expressed by Joanne.
   B. Relate one or more of the inner strengths you possess to the need you perceive in her.
2. *At a diversity training seminar, you are seated next to Harvey Forstman. He seems to be the sort of person you'd like to get to know. The seminar leader asks Forstman if, when approaching others, his inclination is to be factual or to be personal. "I think it's always better to be objective," he replies. "It gives everybody an even break."*

A. Identify the principal need expressed by Harvey.

B. Relate one or more of the inner strengths you possess to the need you perceive in him.

3. *At a Little League board meeting, you sit next to a single parent. She seems terribly agitated by the stern approach to the game taken by some of the managers—discipline, drills, practice. She whispers an aside to you: "Kids make mistakes. I think it is wrong to be too critical of a nine-year-old."*

   A. Identify the principal need expressed by the mother.

   B. Relate one or more of the inner strengths you possess to the need you perceive in her.

4. *It's taken nearly four months to get an appointment with buyer Maynard Miller. He opens the meeting by telling you, "The last person from your company dropped the ball. Never called to let me know there was a problem. I don't like problems. I like surprises even less."*

   A. Identify the principal need expressed by Miller.

   B. Relate one or more of the inner strengths you possess to the need you perceive in him.

5. *The woman immediately ahead of you in the supermarket checkout line glances into your shopping cart. It is filled with packages of chicken, veggies, pasta, and bottled water. Hers, on the other hand, is piled high with junk food and diet colas. "Oh, God," she says, "I seem to buy one of everything that's bad for you. I wish I wasn't so impulsive."*

   A. Identify the principal need expressed by the woman.

   B. Relate one or more of the inner strengths you possess to the need you perceive in her.

6. *It's your first day on the job. Meaghen Kiley, a colleague you've met for the first time, takes you in hand. "Around here," she confides, "hours don't count. All they care about are results."*

   A. Identify the principal need expressed by Meaghen.

   B. Relate one or more of the inner strengths you possess to the need you perceive in her.

7. *You are motoring down I-95 on cruise control. You're tucked behind an 18-wheeler boogeying fast enough to eat up miles yet slow enough to bore the cops. Whoops. The rig peels off into a truck stop. You follow. As you pay your dinner check, the driver wanders over. "Never saw so much radar in all my 21 years on the road," he says. "Don't seem right. I'm no bank robber. All I want is to make a living."*
   A. Identify the principal need expressed by the driver.
   B. Relate one or more of the inner strengths you possess to the need you perceive in him.
8. *You are asked to observe a meeting of the steering committee. The chairperson explains to newcomers, "We try to act with unanimity so we take two votes on every issue. The first determines the position we take. The second gives everyone a chance to be in the majority."*
   A. Identify the principal need expressed by the chairperson.
   B. Relate one or more of the inner strengths you possess to the need you perceive in her.
9. *The cafeteria is exceptionally crowded today. There's one seat open at a small table over in the corner. You ask if you may take it. "Of course," the person replies. "I like surprises."*
   A. Identify the principal need expressed by the person occupying the table.
   B. Relate one or more of the inner strengths you possess to the need you perceive.
10. *Someone from the PR department is assigned to edit your article for the company newsletter. He says, "I'd be happier if you could give the reader fewer facts but more examples of the idea in action."*
    A. Identify the principal need expressed by the PR person.
    B. Relate one or more of the inner strengths you possess to the need you perceive.

WHAT YOUR ANSWERS SAY ABOUT YOU

The point of this exercise is not to see how many right answers you can come up with, because there are no right or wrong answers. Rather, it is to show you that no matter whom you encounter, making yourself valuable to them is as easy as making yourself valuable to you—thinking about yourself in positive terms the other person can understand and relate to.

To extend the benefits of this exercise, pay special attention to the people you encounter daily, strangers and intimates. Mentally figure out how something about you might satisfy something about them. Over time, recognizing other people's needs and formulating an appropriate response to them will become automatic. This is the key to steadily increasing your value and importance to others.

℞4: Do not allow yourself to be the victim of victims.

Roughly 80 percent of the people who fail to steadily improve their value and importance at home and on the job do so for one reason: They do not relate well to others.

The way we relate is essentially a learned response. Whether you are a parent or child, supervisor or manager, secretary or mental health worker, janitor or labor attorney, your most influential teachers were the people who reared you. Note, please, that these people may themselves be poor models of effective communication. They, of course, learned from their parents (who suffered likewise). Seen in this light, the very ways we attempt to relate often mark us victims of victims of victims. This goes a long way to explaining why powerlessness from generation to generation seems so deeply ingrained in some families that it might as well be part of the DNA.

"My mamma and daddy didn't start out to make me a cripple about relating to other people. They tried their best to show me what worked for them," reports Ruth Fornshell, a Phoenix housemaker. "But look, times change. What worked for them doesn't for me, and that's the hardest lesson of all."

I sense in Ruth's experience a warning about the dangers of living an "instead" life:

Instead of choosing how you will act in any given situation, you react.

Instead of coming into an encounter with an open mind, you view life through your legacy of preconceived notions.

Instead of listening with your eyes and your ears to really absorb what other people say, feel, and experience, you distort reality by passing it, unquestioned, through the filter of what you learned subconsciously from your parents. It's like trying to hear a band concert through earplugs.

Instead of empathizing, which might enable you to make informed and sensitive responses, you run on rote.

At the risk of overmaking the point, here's a quick parody of what I mean:

She: I just learned I've got cancer. My dog was struck by a car and the vet says the little guy won't make it. My heart is breaking. The market crashed, I'm broke.

He: That's nice, dear. Did you remember to get my shirts from the laundry?

You get the idea. His response only appears to be harmless. But is that what you are likely to think if you were She? I doubt it. And with good reason. It's really acid. Dissolves any chance of making a meaningful connection before it even starts; eats away at the likelihood of two people coming to the honest meeting of the minds that is the basis for every healthy relationship that was, is, or will be.

Isolation, loneliness, feelings of being misunderstood, family problems, poor work performance, dissatisfaction, psychological stress—no matter what you call it, being a victim is the same as being powerless.

Although you've lived part of your life as a victim of victims, doesn't mean things can't change for the better. They can, and I'll tell you why. Human psychology and practical experience show us that talking and listening—relating to others—isn't like blue eyes. Relating effectively isn't an inherited trait you either have or don't have. No, not at all. In fact, far from it.

It is an undisputed scientific fact that the responses you learned can be unlearned and replaced by new learning. Replacing bad old habits with new and better ones is no tougher than training anybody to do anything. Still, some people say that changing the way they relate can't be done, or that it opens them to needless risk, or that when they try it they sound phoney.

I say they are wrong, dead wrong. I say you can change the way you relate to people, actually improve your life, and still be yourself. In making this statement I do not mean to suggest that changing the inheritance that determines how you interact with others is by any means easy to pull off. It is not. But you should be aware that millions of people's daily lives prove that desirable change is possible. All over the country people like you are taking charge of their lives by taking charge of the way they relate to others.

"I got tired of letting my life happen to me the way it happened to my folks," reports Bates Wildman, from Columbus, Ohio. "That's when I felt I could begin to relate to people, make choices about life instead of operating on autopilot."

Bates's message is this: To be a victim is to deny ourselves the freedom to choose the ways we live our lives. Instead, we settle for the choking constraints of a choiceless way of being. We live used and time-worn lives that rightfully belong to somebody else, not to us.

The practical prescriptions that follow give you three immediately useful ways to improve the way you relate to others while remaining yourself.

℞5: To listen to relate, listen as if you mean it.

Because no one ever teaches us how to listen in ways that contribute to greater understanding between people, we repeat the bad listening habits of our parents.

"My father could look you straight in the eye, but somehow you knew his mind was miles away," reports Zena Medved, a Houston oil company employee. "My mom, on the other hand, pretends to listen but is secretly figuring out what to say given the first opportunity to break in."

These and other bad listening habits lead one smart-aleck to define conversation as a competitive exercise in which the first person to draw a breath is declared the listener.

Wandering eyes, fidgeting fingers, interrupting, asking too many questions—if you see yourself committing any or all of these telltale signs of poor listening on a fairly regular basis, please read on. These are sure to be among the main reasons you fail to develop the relationships that are the foundation of personal power.

THE FOUR BEST WAYS TO LISTEN LIKE YOU MEAN IT

When the following four simple actions become part of your everyday face-to-face contacts, you will automatically listen in a way that relaxes people and makes it safe for them to open up to you.

1. *You must concentrate intensely on the other person.* Communicate your concentration by making eye contact and holding it about 60 percent to 70 percent of the time. Lean towards the other person with an expression of concentration on your face. Keep your hands and body still and relaxed. "Steer" the conversation by saying virtually nothing.
2. *You must focus on what they say, not what you think in response to what they say.* Don't interrupt. Don't jump to conclusions. Wait to speak until you are sure they've spoken their piece.
3. *You must resist asking too many questions.* Frequent questions interrupt the flow. Besides, there's little need for questions when you put more effort into really taking in what's being said than into trying to figure out ways to argue against what the other person is talking about.
4. *You must be alert to gestures and body language.* These messages, which I examine in the next practical prescription, confirm or deny every speaker's words. This secret intelligence helps you make more informed and appropriate responses.

Good listening empowers you to size up people quickly so you'll be able to give them what they want: the facts, the whole story, your feelings, your opinions, an illustration or example, or the pros and cons of a situation.

℞6: Listen with your eyes and act on what you see.

Ever since the serpent sold Eve a bill of goods, words have often proved masks for the truth. Bodies, on the other hand, never lie.

As you read on in this book, you will find a chapter devoted to the all-important subject of body language. Here's a summary of what you'll find there.

It is a scientific fact that people's facial expressions, tone of voice, and postures and gestures give away their truest intentions.

"I'd say much more human communication takes place through body language than verbally," reports Detroit professor of psychology Monique Ward. "Perhaps in the neighborhood of, oh, 60 or 70 percent of understanding is visual. You know, we're all the time picking up and transmitting subtle body movement. Often it's unconscious."

Yes, our bodies unfailingly speak louder than words. When you learn to recognize the signs, learn to listen with your eyes, and act on what you see, you will hear more—even messages people want to hide.

HOW TO READ AND USE BODY LANGUAGE

Here are four steps you must take to gain nonverbal fluency.

1. Concentrate on the main signals. *Facial signals* most accurately reveal what a speaker is feeling. An arched eyebrow, for example, says what you say raises questions in their minds. *Tone and pace of voice* are critical. A slow monotone indicates boredom; a fast, rising tone shows surprise. *Postures, gestures, and movements* are dead giveaways. For example, a crunching handshake is the nonverbal trademark of aggres-

sion. When a person unconsciously leans toward you in conversation, they are signaling interest in what you say.

2. Watch for inconsistencies. When words and body language are at odds, both messages are important. Words tell you what is on their minds, body language says what's in their hearts. It is the truer barometer of what is being communicated. Take notice of the position of people's feet as they talk. When they point directly toward you, you can assume they are comfortable and interested; when they point away, it suggests their minds prefer to be elsewhere.
3. Be especially alert to eye movement. Eyes weep, twinkle, glower, and mourn. They can be shifty or beady . . . and a whole lot more. The point is, with all of their conscious and unconscious movement, eyes tell you what people cannot or will not put into words. By carefully monitoring the eyes of others, you get a handle on the impression you are making. Be alert to rapidly blinking eyes, for instance: They tell you your spoken message isn't getting through. To build rapport, your eyes should meet the other person's about 60 to 70 percent of the time. More may be interpreted as a challenge, less may suggest you have something to hide.
4. Check out clothing, grooming, and the environment. The way we look tells the world who we are, where we stand, and what we think about ourselves. Even if you feel people should not be judged by their clothing, grooming, and environment, these tell a tale. Bright colors, for instance, suggest youth and vitality, grays a more sedate mood. A messy desk doesn't necessarily represent a messy mind; it can also suggest poor time management. Hairstyle, jewelry, attire, furnishings—all of these help us better understand the people with whom we engage.

℞7: Empathize.

The very next time you encounter someone, I want you to imagine what it might be like to say and do and act the way they do. Understand me, please. I am not saying you have to agree with anything. You don't have to condone or condemn their actions or even sympathize. For the moment, just get a feeling of how it might make sense to say what they are saying.

"Seeing people as they see themselves, viewing life from their vantage point, gives me an insight into what's important to them," reports Cephus Bowles, who runs an urban contemporary radio station in Chicago. "This sets me up to position my ideas in terms they can go with."

HOW TO DEVELOP INSTANT EMPATHY

To be empathetic is to be aware of what makes the other fellow the other fellow and not a carbon copy of you. What makes this skill so valuable is that it gets you to see things from their perspective as well as your own. Knowing this, you can tailor what you say to meet both your needs and theirs.

Empathy is a skill you can easily develop. All you've got to do is ask yourself some clarifying questions. The idea is, first, to figure out in your mind what makes them tick, and, second, to present your thoughts accordingly. Here are a few examples of the clarifying questions I have in mind. I hope they'll trigger your thinking and get you to come up with good ones of your own.

- What drives their engine?
  - —Are they more concerned with show or substance?
  - —Do they look up to anybody special?
  - —Do they enjoy life or are they having a hard time?
  - —What do they like and what do they hate?
- How does what they want affect what I want?
  - —Does my thinking create pressure points?
  - —What can I do or say to work around these points?

By mentally raising these and like-minded questions, you cannot fail to heighten the empathy you bring to every encounter. This is certain to help you steadily improve your value and importance to others.

Prescription Recap

Before this chapter comes to an end, I want to briefly headline my seven practical prescriptions—the ones guaranteed to steadily increase your value and importance to others.

℞1: Don't be what you are not.

℞2: Identify and release the real you.

℞3: Speak of who you are in terms of what they want.

℞4: Do not allow yourself to be the victim of victims.

℞5: To listen to relate, listen as if you mean it.

℞6: Listen with your eyes and act on what you see.

℞7: Empathize.

Make success a habit. The way we relate to others is often a matter of habit. Good, bad, or indifferent, our habitual responses—the ones we learned from earliest childhood—are often so much a part of ourselves we do not even notice them. But, by seeing ourselves as we more truly are, and by mentally treating each encounter as if it were the first encounter, we equip ourselves to break the chain of habit that renders us powerless.

Nine Ways to Free Yourself of Self-Defeating Habits and Gain Control of Your Life

Sitting across the desk from Gene Brokaugh, Dave Santini, his boss, was having a hard time trying to figure out if Gene was his best worker or his worst.

"It's obvious from two minutes of conversation that Gene's got more than enough smarts to go far in this organization," reports Dave. "He's got a real quick mind, a good grasp of the technical side, and when he wants to he expresses himself well. The trouble with Gene is that he is so slapdash disorganized. It makes him inconsistent. His poor work habits are a big problem."

Dave thought so highly of one report Gene turned in that he passed it out to other employees and urged them to follow it as a model. "That one gave me the confidence to give Gene a really big assignment, the Sherman report. When he handed it in this morning, it was so awful I called him in on the carpet.

" 'Gene, I'm very dissatisfied with the Sherman report. It's disorganized, it fails to make the key points, and it's so full of sloppy errors I couldn't think of sending it on to upper management. I'd expect work like this from some of the others but, frankly, I know that if you get in the habit of organizing yourself better you'd be the top producer in the unit.'

" 'It's not fair,' Gene responded. 'You pay me what you pay everybody else, but you expect more.'

" 'That's right, I do. I know you can handle it, and when you start meeting my expectations I'll do everything I can to get you the pay raises, promotions, and bonuses you deserve. Meanwhile, here's the Sherman report back. I've made detailed notes in the margins, and I'd like to see your revisions by the close of business on Friday.' "

Success is a habit. But the Gene and Dave story is living proof that so is failure. Habits are part of the unseen emotional baggage we carry through life. Silent and invisible, these come from our past—childhood, school, work experience, you name it! One thing's for sure. Habits are the autopilot that secretly steers most of our thoughts, feelings, and actions—good, bad, and indifferent. And I mean everything from the side we part our hair to the little things that annoy us; from our taste in clothes to the way we deal with job priorities.

What makes a habit a habit is more than rote behavior. We cling to certain ways of thinking and doing and being not just because we've always done it that way but because we think we get something out of it. The gain may be real or imagined, but as long as we feel we gain, we persist. In Gene's case, he'd always been able to get through school and previous jobs with time to spare. He never had to learn the skills of organizing and setting priorities that enable the rest of us to get ahead in life. His bad habits, in other words, prevented him from learning better ones.

Seven Tell-Tale Habits That Rob You of Power

Someone calls your name and you respond. That's a habit. You always say please and thank you. That's a habit. You have a track record of job success. Even that is a habit. But so are the following:

- Disorganization
- Sloppy work habits
- Having a short fuse
- Giving teary responses to stress

- Always seeking the advice of others before making a decision
- Excessive worry
- Blocking things from happening

HOW TO CHANGE YOUR HABITS AND TAKE CONTROL OF YOUR LIFE

Habitual responses are, by definition, independent of what goes on in any given moment. To the degree these blind us to the complete range of options open to us, they quietly, often invisibly, rob our lives of the full measure of joy and happiness that is our human birthright. That is why I intend to show you several truly useful and empowering things in this chapter.

First, I want you to recognize that, in simplest possible terms, choice is power and power is choice. Let me explain. Nobody has the power to exert control over life. What we can control, however, are the responses we make to life's opportunities and events. Accordingly, one of the primary goals of this chapter is to get you to take a look at the habits that secretly prevent you from seeing the options that can lead to personal power and success.

As I have been emphasizing throughout this book, for things to get better in your life, things are going to have to change. Here's the bittersweet part: Habits are the opposite of change. Bad habits are the status quo, endlessly repeated, the predictable chain of cause and effect that can drag you down a highway of tears to the graveyard of hope.

But I don't think it is enough just to see and recognize your hidden habits. You've got to be able to do something about them, find ways to get rid of the bad ones and build up the better ones. This is why I want you to have my nine practical prescriptions. Here you will find no ivory-tower exercises, no excursions in guesswork. Each and every one of my recommendations is the product of 25 years of testing, refinement, and debugging. These are solid, immediately practical, nuts-and-bolts techniques that have helped thousands of men and women. Weave these into your daily doings, make them part of the fabric of your life at home and on the job, and two priceless benefits will light up your life.

1. At work, you will relate better to subordinates, peers, superiors, clients and customers, and the general public. Your achievements will more quickly earn the recognition they deserve.
2. At home, the emotional intimacy between you and the people closest to you in life will deepen to provide a level of personal satisfaction and pride you've never known before.

Self-Test: Are You Trapped by Your Secret Habits?

As you begin to explore the forces of habit that prevent people from getting what they want when they want it, take a quiet, private look at your own habit patterns.

To help you identify the ones that may be getting in the way, I have prepared a simple self-test you will both enjoy and learn from. So sit back, unfasten your seat belt, and read on. See for yourself what, if any, secret habits might be preventing you from growing to the limits of your talent and ability.

Ahead, you will find ten statements. Please read the first one, take a moment or so to reflect on it, then answer the single question that follows. Once you've checked the response that comes closest to the way you feel about what you just read, please go on to the next statement and question. Continue until you have completed all ten. That's all there is to it. As for your answers, I'll discuss the implications as soon as you are done making your choices.

1. Stop and think for a moment about how many secrets you have. Of course, it is often necessary to keep confidences for business or personal reasons. No one is expected to tell everything. But suppose, for instance, you were to reveal to a neighbor, friend, or colleague some detail of your life you had previously withheld. Could something terrible happen?

   ☐ Yes ☐ No

2. You've been brought in to turn around a bad departmental situation: People have been slacking off. You've got a

pretty good idea who the main perpetrators are. You figure there's no point sweet-talking, they'll only take further advantage. Experience shows this to be a situation where the safest course is to trust no one.

☐ Agree ☐ Disagree

3. When confronted with an option you have never considered before—for example, someone asks you to go someplace you've never been—the chances of your saying yes right off the bat are pretty iffy. More likely, you'll probably respond negatively.

   ☐ True ☐ False

4. Think about the gatherings you've gone to in recent months. In general, did you connect with lots of people, including strangers, or was it with a few people you knew beforehand?

   ☐ Many ☐ Same few

5. People come in all colors but only two varieties: the ones who are sensible, and the ones who are . . . well, let's call them more imaginative. Of the two, which are you personally more attracted to:

   ☐ Sensibles ☐ Imaginatives

6. One of your people broke a rule. It produced outstanding business results. Trouble is, someone complained. Now, you've got to decide how to handle the complaint. Here's my question: Is it better to judge your employee by paying more attention to rules than to circumstances, or vice versa?

   ☐ Rules ☐ Circumstance

7. When someone you care about wants something from you, do you prefer to be approached on an emotional basis or is logic always more comfortable to deal with?

   ☐ Logic ☐ Emotions

8. A lot of people take simple pleasure in repeating certain tasks. In your day-to-day life, are you more likely to do things the usual way or do you experiment?

   ☐ Usual way ☐ Experiment

9. You are impatient to get to the heart of a business problem. You need the input of your people, but it's like pulling teeth. How's a manager supposed to turbocharge a Q&A session?
   - ☐ Ask as many questions as possible
   - ☐ Go slow to go fast
10. Some people say that it's okay to interrupt others when they head down the wrong track. And others say that any interruption is a demand on the other person to stop talking and start listening. Where do you come out?
    - ☐ OK to interrupt if warranted
    - ☐ Not OK

WHAT YOUR ANSWERS SAY ABOUT YOU

If your answer to Question 1 was yes, the habit of secretiveness may be preventing you from getting what you want.

As far as Question 2 is concerned, it is well to point out an obvious truth: People in the habit of not trusting are themselves not often trusted.

Your checkmark next to *True,* on Question 3, suggests habitual resistance to change. This keeps your eye so much on caterpillars you miss the butterflies.

If you selected *Same few* as your answer to Question 4, your habit may be to block things from happening in your life—among them the things that might empower you to be the person you always dreamed of becoming.

If you answer Question 5 by saying you prefer to be with sensible people, you should be aware that yours is a potentially blinding habit. It blocks out the view of fresh perspectives—the ones you must heed if you want to prevent your history from being your destiny.

An answer of *Circumstance* to Question 6 indicates a genuine willingness to accept the human condition as a series of sometimes bewildering complications. Hardly an adult alive can honestly say they've never done bad things for good reasons and good things for bad.

People who are in the habit of being excessively logical—of factoring out emotions—as in Question 7—run the worst of all possible risks: Feeling all alone in a crowd. It's an acknowledged fact that roughly 90

percent of the content and meaning of any conversation is emotional. If you tune it out by failing to pay as much attention to nuances as to numbers, you automatically isolate yourself from most of what most people are trying to get across. It's like putting a barbed-wire fence between you and the people you want to or need to be with.

Question 8 presents a curious case: Either answer may indicate the presence of a secret habit. The most practical thing is to strike a comfortable balance between the two that takes into account the needs of the moment.

The habit of asking as many questions as possible, as in Question 9, is the habit of asking too many questions. These slow down the Q&A process.

And finally, Question 10. Interrupting is a terrible habit. It is never justified. It's better to get in the habit of not speaking, even if what they are saying is dead wrong, until they are done. Giving them an opportunity to rattle on and on and on doesn't in any way imply that you agree with what they are saying. Rather, it merely affirms their right to speak hassle-free. In the end, upholding their right will help you get you more of what you want.

How to Turn Bad Habits Into Good Ones

Now that you have completed the self-test, simply note those areas which suggest the presence of a habit that may be doing you more harm than good. Your most pressing problems are likely to lie where your disagreement with my comments is strongest. If you bear these in mind as you read on, you'll discover concrete, specific, and practical ways to make your good habits better and your bad ones invisible.

THE QUICKEST AND BEST WAY TO OVERCOME YOUR RESISTANCE TO CHANGE

Looking back over 25 years of working daily with rising managers at some of America's top corporations, I have two observations that may prove as useful to you as they have to others.

First, no matter what your habit may be, the quickest and best way to get rid of it is to put a better one in its place. This brings me to my second point. I have also developed considerable respect for the resistance a lot of us have to change. When the change is as basic as the way we relate to the people in our lives, it's all the tougher. Still, I am convinced that, if it is possible for people to exchange the habits of booze, drugs, and cigarettes for healthier ones, it is also—and more easily—possible for people to kick the habits that prevent them from getting more of what they want out of life.

"I was so leery about breaking one set of habits and replacing them with another, I didn't even want to hear about it," reports Johnette Rodman, who works for Boeing in Seattle. "I figured I could never be sure change would be an improvement. I told myself, hey, what I got may not be paradise but things could be far worse. Looking back, I can see that avoiding the need for change because I was scared to face the truth is like avoiding the need for an umbrella on a threatening day because you'd really prefer a sunny weather forecast."

Sharing Johnette's experience with you is not intended to make you think change is easy. It's not. What it gets across is that change begins with honest self-acceptance. As I write these words, my hope is that, like Johnette, years from now you'll look back, you'll smile, and you'll wonder what the hemming and hawing was all about.

Practical Prescriptions to Rid Yourself of Hidden Habits

Simply by looking for the choices available to you in any given situation, two things happen. You shove habit on the back burner and you automatically take greater control of your personal destiny.

℞1: Start making choices.

The enemy of habit is choice.

"It's tense on the job. You can't afford to let the population see you in a rut. So you gotta keep things fresh," reports Zena Barnett, who teaches in a prison north of Tucson. "Let's say one of the inmates starts giving me uncalled-for lip. I try to think up three quick and different ways to respond. I can say that I am offended by the disrespect, which I am. Or, I can say that I wondered what I might have done to provoke the sass. Or, let's see . . . I can say that maybe I don't expect perfect discipline but how about showing a reasonable amount of courtesy. The point is that I don't have to respond in the same way every time I am confronted by the sort of problem that comes up again and again in prison classrooms. If I acted by rote, they'd do the same thing over and over until I couldn't take it anymore. So, in every situation, I try to choose the particular way that is going to get the person to safely blow off some steam and leave everybody's ego in one piece."

In prisons as in palaces—in fact, in any and every human encounter—there is always more than one possible way to think, act, and speak. None of these is likely ever to be perfect. That is, none of them is going to get you everything you want. But there's always at least one that's likely to get you more of what you want than the rest. The trick, of course, is to find and choose ones that work for your interests and not against them.

℞2: Develop instant choices by asking, "What else?"

If you have trouble envisioning the options open to you in any particular situation—it could be at work, at home, or out in the community—here's a simple but effective way of handling the problem.

Before you act out of habit, ask yourself, "What else can I do or say or think that will get me more of what I want out of this situation?"

"One of the people who works for me came to complain about unfair treatment on the job. She said that her team leader was having an affair with another employee," reports medical records manager Kendra Jensen, who works in a Houston cancer treatment center. "With this kind of abuse of authority, my first urge was to transfer the leader or to fire him outright—either of which I would've been able to justify. But these steps were sure to hurt the organization's morale and make it harder for me to build a track record of success. So I asked myself, What else can I do to set things right? My choices were to do nothing, talk with the team leader to get the facts and let him know I considered the situation serious, refer the matter to my boss or the personnel people, or take immediate action.

"I decided to talk with him. I found out he was having a relationship all right. Only it was with someone outside the medical center. Case closed."

Next time you find it hard to resist the urge to act out of habit, ask yourself the one question guaranteed to empower you to break the habit of powerlessness: "What else can I do or think or say?" Once you've thought up some options, just decide which ones get you closer to what you want than the rest.

℞3: To change the outcome, change an input.

Habits reflect states of mind.

"One big reason a lot of people feel shy or timid or weak is that these behaviors are often habits of mind. You see, people often have a false picture of what they expect from themselves," reports retired university professor Dr. Donald M. Freytag, who lives near Madison, Wisconsin. "They can't possibly meet their own standards. This leaves them feeling unsuccessful, powerless. But it in no way diminishes their determination to find whatever they think they lack. In fact, the more they lack, the harder they look. They keep on searching for what has not been, isn't going to, and never will, be there. This pattern of searching and failing, searching and failing, is a habit—the habit of being powerless."

Why would anybody endlessly repeat the habits of failure and dissatisfaction?

"Nobody sets out to do it," reported the late Dr. Jules Barron, a nationally recognized authority on pattern behavior. "For example, a spouse stays with a mate who psychologically abuses. Why don't they leave? Because they hope the other will somehow finally come to see that they do not deserve being treated like an emotional doormat. It of course never happens because they unconsciously repeat the pattern that invites being treated like a doormat. The upshot is still more abuse. It's an input-equals-output situation. If you keep on doing the same old things in the same old way, you can't expect the outcome to be any different. The only way to change it is to change what you put into the situation. Cry if you don't ordinarily, and don't if you do; if togetherness is your thing, open a little distance; if abuses are often touched off in the kitchen while cleaning up after dinner, leave the dishes until just before bedtime—anything different to break the otherwise unending cycle of cause and effect."

SMALL CHANGES THAT YIELD BIG RESULTS

Barron's point deserves your best attention. He says breaking pattern behavior requires an understanding that only when you change what you put into situations can you expect new and better outcomes.

"I kept on missing the 7:19 train, grabbed the 7:37 by the skin of my teeth, got to the office a few minutes late," reports commuter Sam Wu, a Baltimore seafood broker. "From the moment the alarm went off at exactly 6:20 A.M., I was behind schedule. The kids take forever on the potty. My wife feeds the baby breakfast, but everyone else free-lances for whatever is easy. There's a line in front of the toaster. My boss called me in one morning. Said, 'Sam, this late stuff is getting to be a bad habit.' Handed me an alarm clock. Suggested I get up just ten minutes earlier, nothing else. It worked. I get the bathroom to myself. There's time for a quiet cup of coffee. I don't miss the sleep. And I'm on the 7:19."

I think you get the idea that to break a bad habit you've got to put a better one in its place. For instance,

- *If your habit is to be untrusting,* try to not count the small change next time you go shopping.
- *If your habit is to be unsure of yourself,* every day for a week make one small decision without first seeking somebody else's advice.

- *If your habit is to act bored,* mentally treat every human encounter on tomorrow's calendar as if it were your first encounter with each individual—be they family members, people you deal with on a daily basis, or strangers.
- *If your habit is failing to set priorities,* make a list of every activity on tomorrow's calendar, then arrange them in order of importance.
- *If your habit is to have a short fuse,* teach yourself to take two deep breaths before you respond to provocation.
- *If your habit is to be disorganized,* next time you write a letter, base it on an outline of the key points you want to make.

Do not worry about faking these or other changes you might make on the ground that they are not the real you. Do them often enough and they will become part of the new you—someone others respect and enjoy being with.

℞4: Look for the real pattern behind the habit.

When it comes to habits, things are not always what they appear to be. For instance, psychologists tell us that when your employees are in the habit of being late, their tardiness may be a cover-up for deep-seated resentment about pressures on the job. It's a relatively mild form of rebellion that diverts attention—yours and theirs—from their underlying anger.

Given the fact that people often mask emotions with habits, it becomes evident why logic doesn't work. Logic, you see, never addresses the real but secret feelings that may be driving the habit in the first place.

"My Pa, he's a reference librarian. He eats facts like I eat popcorn. But, like a lot of Vermonters, he deals with emotions in, well, in unemotional ways. I know Pa loves me but when I was trying to stop smoking the man was my worst enemy," reports ex-smoker Wilhelm Smits, who works for the Small Business Council out of Burlington, Vermont. "I'd get a craving and he'd be there with ten explanations of why it was happening . . . and the logic of breaking the addiction . . . and identifying weak points . . . and this article in *New England Journal of Medicine,* and . . . Oh, please! I didn't want Pa to tell me how to live. At that point I needed someone to tell me that I was going to live!"

Poor Smits. His father means well. But Pa just doesn't understand that his well-intentioned habit of logic only intensifies Wilhelm's suffering. It makes him more acutely aware of, and sensitive to, the pangs and the pain. Some small gesture—maybe something as simple as a friendly arm draped on a temporarily overburdened shoulder—would've been more useful.

Next time you decide to tell yourself or someone else that a habit doesn't make sense, resist the temptation with all you've got. Not only will logic fail, but chances are your personal comfort index will fall so far so fast you'll be forced to drill to find it.

℞5: Just because you feel an old feeling does not mean you need to act on it.

Habits are like the immortal old soldiers of song: They fade but never die.

"At Betty Ford, one of the first things you need to realize is that you can't make old habits disappear. The idea is to be aware of them so you can control them before they sneak up and take hold," reports Los Angelino Raoul Tarrantino, an alumnus of the famous clinic. "Just because you crave something that isn't good for you doesn't mean you have to take it. The feeling never goes away completely. Sooner or later you've got to stare it down. You've got to look the habit in the eye and make it blink. The choice is yours. Say yes to the urge to repeat yesterday's mistakes and you are sure to be worse off than ever before. Say no and you're giving yourself an honest shot at life. It's all about choosing who you want to be."

Raoul is not the first person to recognize that acting on all your feelings is a bad habit that needs to be broken. Albert Camus, winner of the Nobel Prize for literature, shared the view. Only he put it this way: "The hardest thing for some people is not to take what they do not want."

HOW TO DETERMINE WHETHER TO ACT ON A FEELING OR IGNORE IT

Here's a litmus test you can apply in any situation to decide which feelings to act on and which you are better off ignoring: Simply ask yourself, What's likely to happen if I act on this feeling?

- If the answer is negative to your interests, acknowledge the presence of the feeling but do not act on it.
- If the answer is neutral, you are probably better off acknowledging but not acting on it, but it's a judgment call.
- If the answer affects your interests in positive ways, by all means act on it the way political bosses tell their voters to vote—early and often.

℞6: Don't react automatically; focus on what the other person needs.

I want to use the bad habit of interrupting to make a larger point about how to handle bad habits in general.

"Never mind that he was the client. After a while, I got to think of him as the itch I couldn't scratch. For three hours, I'd lay out the groundwork to make a point. But before I could make it, this person would interrupt: 'Let me open a parenthesis on that.'

"It made me furious because he'd then suggest the very idea I was leading up to," reports Natasha Brown-Williamson, a marketing consultant in Lexington, Kentucky. "A couple of months later he got fired. Sends me his résumé. Good luck! I hope whoever eventually hires him teaches him not to interrupt—to wait until the other person's lips stop moving before speaking."

You've experienced it yourself a gazillion times. Kids in the back seat mindlessly interrupting front-seat conversation with, "Are we there yet?" That's a bad habit. Or, the bored civil servant behind the Motor Vehicle wicket who has seen it all (and looks it), and won't let you finish a sentence. That's another bad habit.

Interruption. It's the national sport of the powerless—men and women who need to create the appearance of being in control of the conversation when what they are really doing is playing the pest.

This brings me to the general point I want to make: The underlying problem, psychologists tell us, is being too absorbed with your own rights and concerns to respect those of others. That means one of the quickest and most practical ways to cure bad habits (like interrupting) is to make a conscious effort to shift the focus from your concerns to a broader and more self-empowering concern for everyone's rights and interests.

How to shift the focus from inside to outside

Let's say your lunch partner today spoke of his son's job search, his father's retirement, or his wife's new outlook since Prozac.

- Tonight, take a moment to reflect on what you heard.
- Imagine how things are turning out.
- The next time you see this person, speak about your interest in these matters.

℞7: Slow down.

The habit of impatience indicates an underlying condition called time-sickness.

"I got married on a Tuesday morning at 11:00," reports retired Green Bay Packer quarterback Bart Starr. "I figured that if the marriage didn't work out, I wouldn't blow the whole day."

Starr's sarcasm aside, his point is that the hurry-up state of mind we generate for things worth having comes at the expense of things worth being.

We judge candidates by five-second sound bites. TV news gives us disaster in the time it takes to show a building's collapse. Cars go faster than speed limits allow. Microwaves defrost food at incredible speeds, even though we take many, if not most, meals out.

The time-sickness we suffer affects more than the ways we unconsciously think, behave, and act. It frustrates our desire to be in close and warm contact with others.

ARE YOU TIME-SICK?

Here are the seven surefire signs of time-sickness.

1. You hurry or interrupt the speech of others.
2. Your eyes blink rapidly or fingers tap as others speak.
3. Your body and face are tense.
4. You speak rapidly, drop the ends of sentences.
5. You habitually perform two or more actions at once.
6. You show unreasonable impatience with standing on line.
7. You walk fast, eat fast, and do not linger after a meal.

The presence of two or more of these symptoms indicates an habitual hurry-up state of mind. Read on to discover the steps you can take to cure the habit.

Four fail-safe ways to slow down

The problem and cure are yours to control. Since your response to the pressures of life is the very and only reason you are habitually in a hurry, the cure lies in tearing your mind away from self-absorption. This makes room for a broader and more leisurely view of the feelings and concerns of the people around you, too.

Here are four simple steps sure to produce immediate results:

1. Train yourself to be a better listener. As others speak, do not interrupt. Make eye contact about 60 to 70 percent of the time. Focus more on what is being said than on how you will respond to it.
2. Do one thing at a time. For instance, don't sign checks while speaking on the phone, don't do needlework while listening to someone talk, don't shave while showering.
3. Take five. Every morning around eleven o'clock, give yourself a moment or two to think, meditate, or daydream.

4. Count to ten. Next time you feel like blowing your lid because something or someone's overdue, count to ten. If you still feel mad, count to ten again. Do not act or speak until the urge to blow up passes.

Each of these simple actions—and others you may think of on your own—forces your mind to shed a few activities and thoughts. Do these sufficiently often to ingrain them as habits and you will slow down for sure. As you do, you will find your interest in speed for speed's sake waning. It is the sort of change others will be quick to notice, respond to, and reward.

℞8: Be open-minded about new ideas.

"I asked for and got a transfer because every time I went to my supervisor with a way to improve the flow of work, she'd flat-out reject it," reports telemarketing specialist Norman Feldenkreis. He works for a big publishing outfit in Des Moines. "I guess she figured that if she didn't think it up it couldn't be any good."

Norman's experience is a typical response to what is jokingly known in corporate America as the N.I.H. phenomenon: Not Invented Here. As you know from your own experience, business isn't its only bailiwick. NIH is part of life at home and out in the community, too.

The phenomenon is based on distortion. By distortion I mean attributing to someone or something else what exists only in your mind. It's looking at life through a kaleidoscope and seeing fresh thought as implied but unwarranted criticism.

Actually, NIH in all its various forms is a reliable sign of hidden self-doubt. Because a shaky ego can't stand criticism—real or imagined—it is in the habit of vigilantly being on the lookout for it. All this in the hope that criticism can be located and, if necessary, decoded in time to prevent an emotional trespass.

Obviously, not every idea from someone you work with or live with is going to be valuable or even useful. The problem is to separate the winners from the losers so you can be more discriminating in your response. This is the key to break the habit of shooting down other people's ideas before you know if they're good for you or not.

HOW TO STOP JUDGING AND START BENEFITING FROM OTHER PEOPLE'S IDEAS

Here are three simple techniques you can easily use daily to break the habit of rejecting the thoughts of others out-of-hand.

1. *Get rid of your unwarranted expectations.* When you are about to judge someone's idea, first ask yourself what you expect of the idea and the idea-person behind it. Putting your expectations into words, even if they are unspoken, helps you take a more realistic view of things. You may be expecting too much of the person, the proposal, or both.
2. *View ideas more as opportunities than as problems.* Every good idea "costs" something to implement—time, money, ingenuity, risk . . . something. Not even the best ideas come free. There is always some pain or dislocation in putting them into practice. So the operative question is not whether the idea costs you something to implement but, rather, is the idea worth doing? What it costs is unimportant when the benefits substantially outweigh the charges. Ask yourself the tough questions, not the self-centered ones: Does the idea add value to what presently exists or create new value? Do we have or can we get the necessary resources? Can we afford the benefits?
3. *Evaluate each idea on its own individual merits.* What makes an idea deserving rejection is not the traits it shares in common with other ideas but, rather, its particular flaws. Don't look for reasons to reject an idea because it is in some respects like others you have seen. No, the self-empowering thing to do is to try to find reason to accept it. The key question is this: What makes this particular idea different or better?

℞9: Accept differences; don't demand others do as you do.

"It's not so much that what my boss suggested is wrong. It just came across as a vote of no confidence in my ability to handle the situation," reports Marsh Noyes, who lives and works in St. Louis.

Giving people advice does nobody a favor.

Since you can't possibly understand the full implications of the other person's emotional situation, all you get is the tip of the iceberg. Your superficial approach doesn't address or change what's going on at the bottom of the berg. That's why unsolicited advice is so rejectable, as is (even if secretly) the person giving it.

The key to breaking the habit of offering advice is to stop thinking about life as it is supposed to be and start accepting it as it is.

Face it: Not only do people do things in different ways, they have the right to do things in different ways. Learn to accept these differences. *Accept* isn't the same as *agree with*. You can accept others—allow them to be themselves—without agreeing with what they say or do or think.

Prescription Recap

To close out this all-important chapter about breaking the habits that prevent you from attaining the personal power you desire and deserve, I want you to have a concise summary of its key points:

℞1: Start making choices.

℞2: Develop instant choices by asking, "What else?"

℞3: To change the outcome, change an input.

℞4: Look for the real pattern behind the habit.

℞5: Just because you feel an old feeling does not mean you need to act on it.

℞6: Don't react automatically; focus on what the other person needs.

℞7: Slow down.

℞8: Be open-minded about new ideas.

℞9: Accept differences; don't demand others do as you do.

Ten Ways to Generate the Energy It Takes to Reach Your Goals in Life

"Job hunting is like the movies. The fat guys never get the beautiful girls, and the couch potatoes don't get the offers. Trust me on this. I know what I'm talking about. I was one," reports Jean-Luc Bocuse, who lives in Danbury, Connecticut. A victim of downsizing, after eleven months in limbo Jean-Luc recently landed a slot in pharmaceutical distribution.

"I was on the street for nearly a year. Couldn't figure out how come I didn't connect, I mean with my credentials and all. I made it to the final cut four times but never got an offer."

Then J.L. got lucky. Flying home on the red-eye out of LAX, following another frustrating round of second interviews, he sat next to Evans Robertson. Ev heads up a search team for a Chapel Hill executive recruiting firm.

A couple of hours out, J.L. asked Ev what he was doing wrong. Ev's response surprised J.L.

"Tell me what your day is like. Nitty-gritty stuff. When the alarm goes off, how you feel at the beginning of the day and the end, where you eat, what you wear, the stuff you love and the stuff you hate."

When J.L. finished, Ev thought for a moment.

"You are living proof that the people doing the hiring are like most Americans," Ev said. "We buy the product because we like the package. From what you tell me, no employer could possibly reject you on

job skills. It's the way you present yourself. A little bit overweight, a little bit tired, a little bit of a lazylegs—your personal package is sending the wrong message."

When J.L. protested it didn't seem fair to judge people physically, Ev didn't argue.

"Maybe it isn't," Ev said. "But that's the way it is. Show me two people, one with perfect credentials who looks like a slob and moves like a slug, the other, with sufficient credentials, whose every step says I've got what it takes to go the extra mile. Nine times out of ten the job goes to the person who looks more energetic. And the reason is simple: Savvy as he might be, the first guy doesn't look like he's got enough energy to move the needle. Management jobs are physically demanding. If you slouch your way through the interview, the person on the other side of the desk secretly wonders how you'll handle pressure and long hours."

As they chatted the flight away, J.L. learned that employers go for people who have the knack of walking into a roomful of strangers and giving everyone a fever. It's an invisible glow that wordlessly identifies you as someone who is truly up for the game . . . whatever the game might be.

"I was getting desperate. I couldn't make anything happen. No matter what I did it couldn't get much worse. So what the heck. By the time I got home I decided to give this energy stuff a shot," J.L. says. "I join a racquetball club, find a sensible way to eat to my satisfaction without gaining weight, do a couple of power-breathing exercises in the shower. The first hint I get it's all working is when an old friend says I look taller and trimmer. Six weeks later, I get the offer."

How to Get the Oomph to Make Your Dreams Come True

People believe what they see. That's the moral of Jean-Luc's experience. It lines up with the time-honored belief that personal power is as much about what the messenger appears to be as what the messenger says.

Look, it's simple: Jean-Luc built up the energy it takes to participate fully in his life—on the job and off—and it showed. Thanks to the more confident ways this led him to act, look, and present himself, his vigor convinced at least one employer to make an offer.

To J.L., confidence no longer means coming across like you've got all the answers. Far from it. It means presenting yourself in ways that make people feel like you've got the oomph to make your dreams come true.

An energetic presence goes by many names. Ev calls it a personal package. Others call it aura, magnetism, or charisma. Whatever you may call it, Jean-Luc's, built on quiet energy, telegraphs strength. This attracts the respect of the people he encounters. Their respect makes it easier to get his ideas, thoughts, plans—himself!—across.

Personal power in action—it starts with energy and, if you handle it right, ends by never ending.

THE IMPACT OF ENERGY ON SUCCESS

The energy we bring to our daily lives—the strength with which we act, look, move, and carry ourselves—has a tremendous impact on the people we encounter on the job and socially. It greatly affects how they treat us—fair or foul. It can often make the difference between

- A mistake overlooked and an error that proves fatal
- Respect earned and regard lost
- Love and loneliness
- A career on the way up and a career on the way out

HOW TO CHANGE THE WAY YOU LOOK AND FEEL FOREVER

One of the quickest and best routes to the personal power you want is to develop the energy it takes to be successful in life. The question, of course, is, How?

In the pages immediately ahead, I intend to show you ten big secrets of energetic people . . . the well-springs of physical well-being that enable ordinary people to achieve extraordinary results, turn indifference into attention, conflict into cooperation, rejection into acceptance, distance into warmth, and dreams into reality.

There is nothing blue-sky or ivory-tower about my practical prescriptions. Over the years these have been tested daily by thousands of men and women—people just like you. No matter who you are, my techniques cannot fail to help you find the fuller and more satisfying life you seek.

Step by step, I'll give you honest-to-life examples you can safely follow and be guided by. But amid all of this, there are two things you definitely won't find here: rigorous diet regimens and endless exercise routines.

Instead, I will show you how to quickly master easy-to-learn lifetime skills that will give you a self-renewing source of energy that's yours forever. These will change not just the way you look and feel but the way others perceive you, too.

Apply my ten practical prescriptions to your daily life, become the more energetic person you are capable of becoming in hardly any time at all, and gain these two precious personal benefits:

1. At work, your new physical and emotional reserves will help you go the extra mile, mile after mile—a quality upper management looks for and rewards.
2. Among family and friends, the growing strength of your presence will encourage the people who mean the most to you to take your ideas and feelings into account before making or changing plans.

Self-Test: Do You Know What You Don't Know About Energy?

In no area of life is the relationship between knowledge and power more clearly drawn than in developing the energy it takes to attain your goals in life. The more you know about how to develop energy without killing yourself in a gym or starving yourself, the stronger you can become.

Since this is your first step on the path to knowledge of energy, what you need at this point is a benchmark, one that identifies where you stand and illuminates the areas you need to work on. With that in mind, I've prepared an exercise that's both fun and informative.

What I'd like you to do is really simple. Ahead you will find ten statements. After you read each one, simply put a checkmark next to the response of your choice.

We'll discuss the implications of your personal responses just as soon as you finish all ten.

1. When you inhale deeply, do you feel the elastic waistband of your underpants pressing against your belly?

   ☐ Rarely ☐ Often

2. How many calories are contained in just a single ounce of margarine?

   ☐ More than 200 ☐ Fewer than 200

3. Certain kinds of activities are called aerobic because they deliver oxygen-rich blood to the muscles, where energy burns.

   ☐ True ☐ False

4. Nutrition practitioners agree on very little. Why else would there be so many different diets? But to a person, the one thing they all say is that fat is the enemy: It robs us of energy. Fat, in other words, makes us fatter.

   ☐ Agree ☐ Disagree

5. Regular exercise leaves me tired.

   ☐ Sometimes ☐ Every time

6. When you close your eyes and take a deep breath, can you imagine the positive effect of the breath on, say, your fingertips?

   ☐ Yes ☐ No

7. When someone skinny by nature eats 1,000 calories, they get burned, wasted, somehow used up. Fat people's bodies

are different: They have a great tendency to make as much fat as possible out of the food they eat. This is why, when someone overweight consumes the same number of calories, most but not all of them are used up. The leftovers get stored in the form of fat. The solution for people who fall into this category is not to eat less or to starve. No, it is to get the body to burn up more of the energy contained in the calories consumed.

☐ Agree ☐ Disagree

8. Fifteen minutes of jogging improves oxygen delivery to the muscles as much as three hours of tennis.

   ☐ True ☐ False

9. Better breathing is worth ten IQ points.

   ☐ Agree ☐ Disagree

10. Small amounts of fatty food contain more calories than large amounts of lean food. Accordingly, through careful selection, it is possible to eat more without gaining any weight at all.

    ☐ Fact ☐ Fiction

WHAT YOUR ANSWERS SAY ABOUT YOU

If your answer to Question 1 is that you rarely feel the elastic expanding as you inhale, it is probably because you are breathing from your chest instead of from where it will do you the most good—from the depths of your gut. Shallow breathing fails to expand the lungs fully. It works like a choke-collar. You get enough oxygen to survive but not enough to thrive.

Insofar as your reply to Question 2, what you need to know is this: 1 ounce of fat contains 255 calories, no matter if that fat is butter, margarine, olive oil, Vaseline, or bear grease. Meanwhile, an ounce of protein or an ounce of carbohydrate has less than half the calories. Said another way, by selecting generous amounts of protein and of carbohydrates but not of fat, not only can you eat more, you can actually burn up some of the body fat you started with.

Aerobics, the subject of Question 3, is one of those things that nobody can fully explain but whose benefits everyone agrees on. The acknowledged basics are these: Muscles—and by muscles I mean more than your biceps. I also mean the ones in your arteries, veins, and vital organs—work all the time without your being aware of them. They all need oxygen to function. Without this clear, odorless, and invisible gas that makes life possible, they are unable to take full advantage of the fuel contained in the calories you eat. The more energy muscles produce, the more oxygen they must have. Aerobic activities train your system to use as much natural oxygen as your muscles can safely handle. Done properly, following professional medical advice, these activities burn off calories in a safe way. For an added plus, they produce a pleasant feeling of well-being in most people.

As for Question 4, professionals will tell you that, ounce for ounce, eating fat makes people fatter than if they ate protein or carbohydrates. Most people aren't so much overweight as they are overfat. Here's an example: As inactive professional football players age, their unused muscles turn to fat. They may be the same weight as in their prime, but now their weight is the sum of more fat and less muscle than ever. You can't call them overweight. No, they are overfat.

If, at the end of reasonable aerobic activity—dancing, walking, jogging, jumping rope, racquetball, cycling, swimming, skating, and so on—you nearly always feel more tired than refreshed, your answer to Question 5 should be taken as a warning. It says you must be doing something wrong. Within a week or so, most people find regular activity doesn't use energy so much as make it.

The basis for Question 6 is a simple idea: By making breathing more of a conscious act, we train our bodies to breath better. The effect of actually experiencing oxygen as it courses through the blood is empowering. In the pages ahead, I will show you three ways to do it.

If you deny or have a hard time accepting why skinny people stay skinny while fat folks tend to get fatter (Question 7), I suggest you read this chapter with great care. The information ahead is certain to open your eyes to just how easy and sensible it is to be more energetic. Nothing in these pages is idle speculation or a matter of opinion. What you will learn is confirmed by the best thinking of the world's leading physiologists.

Question 8 is really intended to open your eyes to a couple of concepts. First, you don't have to run a marathon to get the oxygen benefits of aerobic activity. Walking. Jumping rope. Running in place. Dance aerobics. The list goes on and on, and you are free to choose any or all of them. The activities you choose will probably depend on your doctor's say-so and how much time you have. For instance, if you can play hard tennis for several hours a day every day, that's fine. If time presses, you might want to consider a 12-minute jog. They are equally beneficial.

Among the organs of the body most favorably affected by the presence of oxygen (Question 9) is the brain. An oxygen-rich blood supply quickly restores and stimulates wakefulness, alertness, and the ability to absorb and integrate information. That's one reason why you see so very many professional football players take oxygen the moment they hit the bench.

Setting out on a lifelong energy buildup (Question 10) means making choices every step of the way. The mere fact that you are reading these words tells me you have already made the first and most important one: Do you want to take charge of your life, eat more, breathe better, and grow your energy . . . or are you content to eat less, choke-off the vital flow of oxygen, and lose vitality?

Now that you have completed the exercise, please note those areas where your knowledge is less than complete. If you will bear these in mind as you read forward, you'll discover concrete, specific, and useful ways to develop energy you can use to awaken the power and confidence within.

WHERE YOUR ENERGY COMES FROM

In a moment, I want to give you my ten practical prescriptions for energy. First, though, it's a good idea for us to briefly go over some basics.

Energy is an ongoing process, not a one-shot event

When you look at a sheer rock wall hundreds of feet high, it appears impossible to scale. Yet climbers do it all of the time. They reach the top by breaking the climb into segments. Then break down each segment to specific handholds, develop handholds into footholds. Like itsy-bitsy spiders in a rainspout, they steadily inch their way to the top.

The same is true of developing the energy it takes to get what you want out of living. If you tell yourself to go out and hustle up some more energy, you're up against a sheer rock wall. But if you break it down to its elements, make each part of an ongoing, step-by-step process, your personal toehold on energy cannot fail to quickly build to a stronghold.

Getting rid of useless body fat is one part of the process

Only muscles produce energy. Whether you are fat or fit, tall or short, or come in any of a rainbow of colors, your entire circulatory system—heart, lungs, arteries, veins, and capillaries—is built to transport oxygen-rich blood to the muscles, where energy comes alive.

Let me quickly explain why this is the case. You see, no matter what you eat, the body converts most of the calories you consume into fat. Roughly 70 to 80 percent of the fuel your muscles need has to be in the form of fat molecules. These are either burned off to meet the muscles' immediate needs or, when they are in oversupply, stored away as body fat. If the last meal you consumed contained less fat than your muscles need, your body draws on its reserves; if it contained an excess, it is stored. If you can avoid taking in fat, your body has no choice but to draw from stored reserves. This makes avoiding dietary fat the quickest, easiest, and safest way to get rid of useless body fat.

Oxygen, the raw material of life, is another key to building human energy. It is a physiological fact that human energy is always directly proportional to the body's ability to uptake and use oxygen efficiently. Think of it this way: You can live weeks without food. A few days without water. But five minutes without oxygen threatens life itself.

Why your energy depends on how much oxygen you burn

People with highly efficient oxygen-delivery systems invariably burn more energy than those whose circulation is at a lower state of fitness. Said another way, the more energy you wish to burn, the more oxygen you need to burn it. If you can find ways to increase your body's ability to acquire and utilize oxygen, you can easily and, perhaps, substantially, increase your personal energy—no matter what your age, weight, or level of fitness.

In saying this I do not mean to imply that more oxygen turns 90-year-olds into athletes. I am not saying that at all. My point is that more and better use of oxygen cannot possibly fail to raise energy levels of people from nine to 90—and even older. If you are breathing, your body needs all the natural oxygen it can get—not to create a new you but to improve the you you are.

If you are in health care, oxygen will give you the stamina to meet any emergency. If you are in government, oxygen reserves will prove enough to overcome the nightmare of bureaucracy. If you are a jogger, you'll be amazed by the power of oxygen to drop your pulse as you quicken your pace.

HOW TO LIVE, EAT, AND BREATHE FOR ENERGY

There are three main routes to improve our ability to obtain and make use of natural oxygen. These are:

1. Improve breathing to get more oxygen.
2. Eat to make the best use of oxygen.
3. Train our bodies to burn more oxygen, and at higher rates.

PRACTICAL PRESCRIPTIONS TO GENERATE THE ENERGY YOU NEED TO REACH YOUR GOALS

I can't say that building up your energy is a bed of roses. There are times when the best of us would rather put up our feet and dream of a magic way to tone our muscles and enhance our capacity for oxygen. By if you follow my practical prescriptions, I can assure you that you will join those of us who are proud to be getting the most out of the bodies we were given.

℞1: Don't save your breath.

"The reason you can't expect more energy without breathing more oxygen is the same reason you can't burn logs in your fireplace without opening the flue damper," reports respiration therapist Theola Warbank, who works in a hospital near Hot Springs, Arkansas. "Food that's been converted mostly to fat gets 'burned' with oxygen to release energy. It works like fuel oil. Most of us are born with more capacity for oxygen than we normally make use of. So it's a use-it-or-lose-it situation."

"Use it or lose it" is an idea most often applied to muscle function. Absent the steady use that comes with exercise, heart muscles, for instance, lose their pumping efficiency. But with it, efficiency not only returns, it can be improved—even for victims of heart attack. As much can be said for breathing. Most of us pay little or no attention to the breath. As a consequence, we inhale only enough air to get by—about one and a quarter gallons of air a minute—though our natural capacity can be as much as 26 gallons a minute.

Obviously there is an in-between point at which you benefit from increased oxygen flow without the huff and puff of overdoing things. There is no one "right" amount of oxygen for all individuals. Each person's need is different, and it's up to you to find your own comfort level. However, there's one and only one way to work toward finding that point. And that is to become more fully aware of the breath as it passes into and out of your body.

THE ONE-MINUTE-A-DAY ULTIMATE BODY CONDITIONER

Here is one of the easiest and most enjoyable ways to build the energy you need for success.

1. Make yourself comfortable, close your eyes, and simply breathe normally. Focus your mind on the breath. Let yourself become fully aware of the ebb and flow of air.

2. When you are completely relaxed, pay close attention to one breath cycle. Experience the slow movement of air from the first of the in-breath to the last of the out-breath.
3. Repeat step 2 ten times.

As you make this simple but powerful exercise part of your daily routine—ten breaths take less than a minute—you will subconsciously become more aware of breathing. Over time, this inner awareness will automatically lead your body to breathe better.

The resulting increase of oxygen is the ultimate body conditioner. It instantly helps you feel fresher and better able to handle whatever comes along. In moments of tension, when you need all the energy you can muster, it can be a godsend.

℞2: Inflate your body, not just your lungs.

Try this experiment:

First, take a shallow breath from the top of your lungs. When you've released it, breathe once again. But this time make it a deeper breath. Start breathing from around your navel. Bring the breath up from there, letting it rise into your chest.

If you are like most people, you'll notice that the second breath seems to deliver an oxygen rush. It raises your body, lifts it in the same way a rubber raft inflates—growing truer to its full promise with each molecule of added air.

This quick little experiment should lead you to make a couple of very pleasant discoveries. First, you'll love the feeling of opening up your body to the power of maximum oxygen. Second, you'll experience an instant of physical vitality you'll want to repeat again and again.

Am I suggesting you breathe from deep in your gut all of the time? Of course not. What I am saying is this: Under normal conditions, we breathe roughly 2,000 gallons of air a day. Anything you can do to increase oxygen flow is sure to bring you closer to the levels of energy and fitness you desire.

THE TWO-MINUTE-A-DAY PICK-ME-UP

Here is one of the best and simplest ways to get more of the oxygen your muscles need for the energy, endurance, and vitality it takes to live life to the fullest. Start-to-finish, the entire exercise takes less than two minutes a day.

1. When seated comfortably, fully deflate your body by exhaling completely to a count of ten.
2. As air leaves, bend from the waist to bring your forehead as close to your knees as you can. If you can't make it all the way to your knees, that's okay. Go as far as you comfortably can.
3. Now, reverse the process. Inflate your body to a count of ten. As air steadily enters, slowly raise your shoulders to bring your body to its fully erect, seated posture.
4. Repeat the cycle five times.

℞3: Feel your fingers breathe.

"If you can see it in your mind and feel it in your heart, it can be," the Rev. Jesse Jackson is quoted as saying. Though he was talking about success in general terms, his words have particular relevance to the subject of energy-building success. Jackson's language says that the attitude we bring to a situation foretells our experience of it. Here's the tie-in: By imagining the experience of breath on various parts of the body we actually teach ourselves to sense and recognize the effect of it.

"First time I sensed my fingers breathe was a new experience," reports Sean Johnson, who brokers industrial real estate in Albuquerque. "I know it sounds like a survivor of the 1960s talking but, honest, I really felt my fingers tingle a little bit with each breath, and now I can do it all over, any time I want to—sitting at my desk, driving, playing golf, anywhere."

By learning to experience the physical effects of the breath, Johnson monitors his body's total readiness to produce all the energy he needs to meet his goals and satisfy his desires.

YOUR WHOLE-BODY BREATHING PLAN

It takes time to fully experience the effect of the breath on various parts of the body. Thankfully, it's one of those circular notions: the more you experience, the more you are able to experience. How long it takes you will depend on two things: the care with which you perform the following exercise, and how often you do it.

1. Sit in a comfortable chair in a quiet setting. Close your eyes and breathe normally.
2. Try not to think too much. Simply experience the feeling of the air moving in and out of your lungs.
3. Allow yourself to wonder what the flow of oxygen feels like in, say, your throat or your right knee, or whatever. Do not strain to feel what you wonder. Simply allow the question, whatever it is, to be: Does oxygen soften my lips? Does it release strain in my upper back? Does it put more feeling back into my toes?

Persist with this exercise, rehearse it every day if only for a minute or two. The results are more than worth any minor effort it takes.

℞4: Don't eat less, eat smarter.

"I was born a candidate for a heart attack or stroke. My father died of his ninth—yes, ninth!—heart attack at the age of 62. My mother's third proved fatal. And both my sisters have coronary artery disease," reports San Francisco wine importer Danilus Altmann. "Though the genetic deck is still stacked against me, I've lost 20 pounds, dropped my cholesterol 57 points—all without going on a diet. I just taught myself to eat smarter, not less. I still take in about 2,200 calories a day, only now they're helping me burn fat to release more energy."

A diet is a decision. No deviations. You must eat exactly two of these for breakfast and three of those for lunch. What makes this practical prescription valuable is what makes it different. No rigid diets. Just choices. A do-it-yourself way to eat more, realize more energy—at the same time you burn off excess body fat. That's right. Choose satisfying quantities of foods rich in the proteins and carbohydrates that nourish muscles, burn off more energy with better breathing and sensible aerobics that fit your personal lifestyle, and you can bet the farm that, as your energy grows, the inches will melt away.

- Love handles will be little more than memories.
- A trimmer waistline is yours.
- Cellulite won't be the problem it once was.
- Your energy level will tell people you look and feel like the winner you are.

℞5: Eliminate excess dietary fat.

"If you wouldn't bathe table corn, which has a high fat content to begin with, in motor oil, why in the world would you bathe it in butter? Butter, motor oil—call it any name you like, it's all pure grease," reports Edna Ohbermeyer, who runs a Nashville insurance company's executive dining room.

Ounce for ounce, fat delivers more than twice as many calories as protein or carbohydrate. Fat makes you fat because you get too many calories out of too little food. So little, in fact, you think nothing of that second pat of butter or extra dollop of sour cream. A pat here, a dollop there . . . before you know it, you're talking half sizes and the big-and-tall department. So it figures, the more fat you take in or have, the more oxygen you need to burn it off in energy.

According to fitness expert Covert Bailey, indolent people tend to be overly proficient at converting food to fat and storing it, and have a less-than-normal proficiency for burning it. So, what happens to all those unoxidized calories? They're stored as fat. Most of us have enough stored fat to take care of our energy needs without taking in more. If you reduce the intake of fat to below what your muscles require, you automatically convert stored body fat to energy.

It matters not at all how you eliminate most of the fat in your diet, but eliminate it you must if your goal is to increase your energy. In ℞7, I'll show you one easy way that's proved highly effective. But first, let me make the point that even if you stopped eating all the fat you know about, you'd still be getting all the fat your body needs.

Fat is hidden in food you would never suspect it to be in. Sixty percent of the calories in a handful of peanuts come from fat. Frankfurters deliver 75 percent. Anything made with whole eggs is nearly as much. The source of 30 to 40 percent of pizza calories is fat. A big baked Idaho potato is roughly 140 calories plain but nearly 400 calories when dressed in butter and cream. A mouthful of steak—a reservoir of fat if there ever was one—has five times the calories of a mouthful of pasta.

Let me be perfectly clear on this point. Fat is the enemy and it doesn't matter what kind of fat it is. For instance, if you stop eating steak or butter in favor of nuts or olive oil, you are trading one bad choice for another bad choice. Animal or vegetable, they're all 100 percent fat. The important thing is not where it comes from. The important thing is first to take in less of it, and second, to burn off more of it.

People are sometimes reluctant to give up most dietary fat because they associate the giving up with a feeling of deprivation. But if you just give it a try, you'll find it isn't at all hard to do. For instance, instead of eating a pint of premium ice cream every night, eat a pint of your favorite frozen, fat-free yogurt. There's no sacrifice in that.

℞6: Get more of what you like by taking less of what you don't need.

"Diets work. I ate grapefruit and lost 20 pounds. I drank alcohol and I lost weight. Of course they work, but only while you are on them," reports Lillian McWhortle, a fire department dispatcher in Oklahoma City. "Diets don't fail. Dieters do."

The reason dieters fail—lose motivation—is a matter of choice. Let me quickly explain by saying that, somehow, even when the options are dark, darker, and so dark you wouldn't believe it, the feeling that you are entitled to choose among them is always more humanly empowering than being forced to follow a rigid rule.

According to several highly respected university studies, people denied the freedom to make choices in weight management programs experience feelings of being deprived. They find it hard to enjoy themselves. After a while, they begin to feel like life's closing in on them. They plague themselves with questions that begin with words to the effect of "Why me?" Everything associated with food ends up a misery. Eventually, they just can't take it any more and they quit.

Your best shot at building the energy you want is to avoid anything that locks you into a rigid food regimen. That's why I developed the following chart. It shows you how easy it is to eat all you want, build the energy you need, and burn off stored up body fat—all at the same time.

Notice the chart is divided into four food groups you must eat to get balanced nutrition. Within each of those categories I've listed specific kinds of foods under three headings—desirable, less desirable, least desirable.

The chart is constructed to put food with high fat content on the extreme right-hand side, food with little or no fat content on the left. Simply by avoiding the kinds of food listed on the right, you give oxygen a chance to work on the fat that marbles your muscles and sheathes your middle.

Ice cream. Butter. Cookies. Pork, beef, nuts, and avocados. These seem a small price to pay for the richness and variety available to you on the rest of the table.

But don't get me wrong. I don't want you to feel hungry. In fact, I want you to eat as many calories as your lifestyle demands. It doesn't really matter if you are a marathoner packing in 4,000 calories a day or a fashion model trying to hold it down to 1,500. Just make sure that those calories all come from food on the left side of the table.

	Desirable	Less Desirable	Least Desirable
Milk products	non-fat milk non-fat yogurt farmer's cheese	2% milk part-skim ricotta	ice cream butter cream cheese
Grains and cereals	whole grains	pasta	Oreos
Meat, meat substitutes	beans brown rice tofu	white rice chicken flounder fillet	pork beef nuts
Fruits and vegetables	most unprocessed fruit and vegetables		avocado olives

℞7: Train your muscles; create more energy.

There's one and only one way energy comes alive: It's in the muscles, where calories burn with oxygen. Accordingly, the fastest, best, and only way to create a tremendous amount of sustained energy is to train your muscles to use more oxygen.

The most efficient exercises for this purpose are called *aerobics*. Let me tell you why they work. Aerobics means steady exercise that demands an uninterrupted output from your muscles sufficient to attain an exercise pulse—which you'll be reading more about in a moment.

We've already agreed that muscles need oxygen to produce energy. The harder you work them, the more oxygen they need. As you exercise steadily and without interruption, your heart rate goes faster and faster as your body pumps in more and more oxygen to meet demand. How fast is enough? The answer depends on your age and general physical condition. That's why I strongly urge you to consult your health care professional before you start aerobics.

HOW FAST YOUR HEART SHOULD BEAT DURING AEROBICS

Assuming your health care professional advises one or another form of aerobics, you should exercise hard enough to get your heart steadily going at 80 percent of its maximum, for 12 minutes, three or more times a week.

Maximum heart rate is a theoretical number related to age. To determine yours, simply subtract your age from 220, and multiply the result by .80.

Let's walk through a couple of examples:

- A forty-year-old should exercise continuously at a steady pulse of 144.

  220 – 40 = 180 × .80 = 144
- A 20-year-old should exercise continuously at a steady pulse of 160.

  220 – 20 = 200 × .80 = 160

It's a mistake to think that you need to run a foot race or dance your head off to be aerobic. All you've got to do is walk, jog, run, dance, whatever, fast enough to get your heart going at the correct beat for a person of your age. This safely and automatically conditions your muscles to burn more oxygen at higher rates, and trains your body to produce more energy—not just while you work out but for several hours after activity is completed.

℞8: Make haste slowly.

Is it a good idea for people out of shape to do 12 minutes of aerobic activity right from the start? The answer is yes, but . . .

Yes, in the sense that laboratory studies the world over agree that 12 minutes of steady, uninterrupted exercise is what it takes to build up the capacity of your muscles to use oxygen for energy. If, however, you are terribly out of shape and find it difficult to maintain a heart rate that's 80 percent of capacity for 12 full minutes, start out at between 60 and 70 percent maximum heart rate for a few weeks. When the aerobic activity of choice seems to require less effort, that's the time to increase intensity gradually until you reach 80 percent. In any case, you should sustain 12 minutes right from the getgo.

It is neither necessary nor desirable to be exhausted to achieve an improvement in energy levels. Make haste slowly and, over time, you will notice improvement.

℞9: Choose aerobic activities you enjoy most.

"I gave up after a week, and what a mistake that was," reports Harry Doyle, a Tampa businessman. Harry had chosen jumping rope for his aerobic activity. It was cheap. He could do it day or night, rain or shine, on a business trip or at home. Though he had never done it before, he figured it was worth a few minutes on the learning curve.

"But my pulse went through the roof. I got so tired after four or five minutes I stopped. I did that for five days straight, figured it wasn't working, and quit."

I don't know what Harry's pulse might have been during those four or five minutes, but it was probably higher than it should have been. I am glad Harry showed the good sense to stop before he hurt himself.

Instead of exercising at a heart rate appropriate for his age, one that, over time, would produce new fountains of energy, Harry's choice—jumping rope—drained Harry's stamina. No wonder he didn't enjoy himself. Wouldn't you quit, too?

Eventually, I got my friend Harry to try riding a stationary bike. The idea sold itself in nothing flat when he realized it gave him a chance to get a workout at the same time he read those business reports he never had enough time to get to before. "It's a double double-whammy. Not only do I build up energy while I am getting more work done, riding the bike inside gets me in shape to enjoy family bicycle excursions on the weekend."

Here's my take on Harry's experience: It's human nature not to want to do what we do not like. Harry disliked jumping rope. So he upped and quit. Meanwhile, Harry loves the stationary bike so much he builds it into his lifestyle. The payoff? He enjoys getting the energy boost his active lifestyle—business and personal—demands.

THE BEST WAY FOR A BEGINNER TO GET A JUMPSTART ON ENERGY

Any activity that safely causes your heart rate to reach and, for 12 minutes, sustain 80 percent of its theoretical capacity confers aerobic benefits. If you do it by walking, fine. Perhaps a class in dance aerobics is your thing. That's okay, too. The important thing is not which ones you choose, but to select the ones you enjoy. So, for heaven's sake, don't feel you have to hang in with an activity you don't like. Just choose another one.

Generally speaking, activities that continuously engage large masses of muscle—walking, stair-climbing, cycling, jogging, swimming, dancing, cross-country skiing, and the like—demand the most oxygen because they burn the most fat. Doing these on a regular basis amounts to a jumpstart on life. Even better news, they produce their quickest and most dramatic results among beginners.

℞10: Monitor your pulse.

Most men have a resting pulse of about 72; most women average about 80. As you train your muscles to burn oxygen more and more efficiently, your resting pulse will drop. Very athletic people come in as low as 35. But no matter what your resting pulse, *never, ever drive your exercise pulse rate above 80 percent of its theoretical maximum.*

Be sure to check your pulse often. When you first start aerobic activity, you may have to stop a few times to be sure you are not exceeding safe pulse limits. After a while, when you know what the correct heart rate feels like, you should be able to do the 12 minutes nonstop and check it only when you are done.

How to take your pulse

1. Don't take your pulse with your thumb. It has its own pulse and may lead to a double count.

2. Find your pulse on the thumb-side of your wrist or the side of your neck. Lay your fingertips on the area. One of your fingers will pick it up.
3. Once you find it, count it for exactly six seconds. Multiply the number of beats you count by 10.

PRESCRIPTION RECAP

Now that we have covered my ten practical prescriptions, I'd like to briefly recap them for you.

℞ 1: Don't save your breath.
℞ 2: Inflate your body, not just your lungs.
℞ 3: Feel your fingers breathe.
℞ 4: Don't eat less, eat smarter.
℞ 5: Eliminate excess dietary fat.
℞ 6: Get more of what you like by taking less of what you don't need.
℞ 7: Train your muscles; create more energy.
℞ 8: Make haste slowly.
℞ 9: Choose aerobic activities you enjoy most.
℞10: Monitor your pulse.

Personal power relies on more than the psychological feeling that we are going to succeed because we are now more resourceful and more capable than ever. Important as these are to have and to hold, inner thoughts and emotions alone aren't enough. They can't communicate power. If they did, nerds would be kings. No, these need a catalyst—something that credibly projects the inner confidence we may be experiencing.

That catalyst is the energy we bring to life—the vigorous way we carry ourselves, move, act, and interact. When we've got the energy it takes to attain our goals in life, we transmit a clear but unspoken signal of self-confidence that others find easy to receive, understand, and accept. We appear to others to be comfortable in the physical and emotional space we occupy. This seamless ease with which our emotional and physical selves co-exist is an unmistakable signal. It tells the world we've got what it takes to make our dreams come true.

Sixteen Ways to Change Your Life By Changing the Way You Dress

". . . and my advice is never dress up, never dress down, simply dress level."

Rene Proskower was fascinated. "I've heard about dressing up and down but I've never heard anyone talk about dressing level. What does it mean?"

Business consultant Nick Coltrane smiled. "Maybe I've added a term to our language," he continued jokingly. "What I mean is this: If you want to be a leader in your field, the last thing you want to do is dress up in something that is striking, different, or unique, or dress down in something so casual it draws attention away from what you have to offer. To be thought of as a leader you want to wear what leaders wear when they lead."

Rene asked Nick to elaborate.

"Fashion attracts attention, but it doesn't project power," Nick went on. "True leaders—not the wannabes but the real McCoy—they don't want to attract attention to their clothing, they want people to concentrate on them, not what they're using to cover their bodies."

Nick offered to prove his point. He asked Rene to close her eyes. "We've been talking for 10 minutes. Can you describe in detail the suit I am wearing? What color is it? Is it striped, solid, plaid, or tweed? What about my shirt, my tie? Tell me about my shoes. How many rings am I wearing?"

With each question, Rene found herself guessing at the correct answers. It amazed her to realize she was talking to someone about the part dress plays—and had hardly noticed what he was wearing.

Nick had proved his point: By dressing level, other people paid more attention to what he had to say than to what he had on.

The moral of the story is simply this. The impression your wardrobe creates either attracts power by allowing your best personal qualities to shine through or it makes the growth and development of your personal power, confidence, and leadership potential impossible.

Self-Test: Do You Need to Read This Chapter?

Answer yes or no to the following questions.

1. Have you ever been turned down for a promotion or a raise you honestly deserved?
2. When you meet people or see them for the first time, do you ever get the feeling you fail to instantly command their favorable attention, confidence, and respect?
3. Do you feel it is unfair to be judged—and to judge others—by their appearance?
4. Do you select your working wardrobe on the basis of low price or to personally please a certain someone of the opposite sex?
5. Do you dress more for the job you have than for the one you want?

WHAT YOUR ANSWERS SAY ABOUT YOU

If even one of your answers is yes, the way you dress is probably working against your personal and career interests instead of enhancing them. Not to worry—there's a bright side to the picture.

No matter what your gender, no matter who your employer, no matter which part of the country you live and work in, reading this chapter will give you dozens of specific, concrete, and workable ways to change your life simply by changing your appearance for the better.

How to Dress Smart

Right off the bat, I want to set your mind at ease. When I say "change your appearance for the better" I am not talking about twisting your arm into giving up your personal taste. Neither am I prescribing some kind of a cookie-cutter look that immediately identifies you as more of a follower than a leader.

What we're talking about here is focusing your personal selections—the expression of your taste—in ways that both please you and give your career the extra leverage it needs to get you to where you want to go. More good news: Since a little forethought can make every dollar deliver 40, 50, even 60 percent more value, you don't have to spend a fortune to dress smart.

WHAT YOUR CLOTHES SAY ABOUT YOU

Your next promotion may depend as much on what's in your closet as what's in your head. I say this because it is a fact of life that your clothes never lie. The story they reveal tells people in a glance what words alone cannot convey:

- Your present economic level
- Your capacity for success
- Your social skills
- Most important, your promotability

"To give you an idea of how important top management regards the subject of dressing for success, several of the *Fortune* 500 CEOs

I represent have clothing allowances built into their compensation packages," reports Certified Public Accountant Timothy F. Flagler IV, who practices out of offices in Palm Beach, Florida, and Lake Placid, New York. "It's justified on the same grounds that the expense of corporate advertising is justified. Clothing and appearance are critical to the way Corporate America wants to present itself, how it wants its people to be seen by the public at large, especially the people and organizations it does business with."

Like Tim's upper management clients, you are forever in the position of having to sell yourself and your ideas to colleagues and socially. Part of selling yourself has to do with the way you dress. My point is simple: If some of the most successful people in the country believe the care, concern, and cash invested in wardrobe favorably impacts their corporate and personal destinies, who are you to argue? Just follow their lead—take advantage of the fact that insofar as the world is concerned, you are what you wear—and you cannot possibly fail.

WHY TOP EXECS DRESS THE WAY THEY DO

Working with various leading managements over the years, I've noticed that, in any one organization, the top echelon seems to dress in similar ways. Whatever the look—jeans and sneakers at a Silicon Valley think tank, or dark suits and well-shined tassel-ties in a Wall Street law firm—it doesn't happen by accident. Actually, it's a form of communication:

- Their clothes tell their colleagues they belong.
- To be accepted in their world, your wardrobe must get across the idea that you belong among them.

HOW TO OPEN NEW VISTAS OF BUSINESS AND SOCIAL SUCCESS

Have you ever noticed how some people can command an entire room with their look and style? How they have the knack of wearing the business clothes that strike just the right note for the occasion—be it a golf outing to build working relationships or a negotiating session to build the business. They seem to dress for success almost effortlessly.

I'll let you in on a secret: These folks don't have anything you lack in the way of personal charisma or natural talent. Sure, they've got the wardrobe, but that's only the tip of the iceberg, the part you see. Underneath, invisible, lie a handful of even more valuable skills and strategies, the driving forces that are the foundation of their wardrobe success. A command of these is like having a team of your own personal tailors and fashion consultants to guide your every stitch—what you wear and what you buy. You'll be relieved to know these skills can be mastered with ease to build a wardrobe that works as hard and as long as you do.

Each of the sixteen practical prescriptions I give you in the pages immediately ahead is the real thing, used by career-minded people like you to dress their way to the top everywhere they go. Each technique produces spectacular results. Put these to work daily and you will gain three powerful career benefits:

1. Suddenly, people who once ignored you will be intrigued by your views and ideas. Men and women who might once have dissed you out of hand will now give you their unqualified support.
2. Your business and social horizons will expand beyond your wildest dreams, and barriers to professional advancement will fall away as adversaries turn into loyal allies.
3. Imagine the thrill of walking into a room full of strangers and quickly and easily becoming the focus of everyone's favorable attention.

Practical Prescriptions for Creating the Right Image

To help you project quiet influence and power, my sixteen tested techniques will show you, step by step, how to use your appearance to achieve your goals and in the process actually change your life by helping you become the person you want to be.

℞1: To make your appearance work for you, think before you dress.

"I am sitting in my office waiting for a guy I met at a bass fishing camp in the Ozarks, a civil engineer. He's in town for the day. I invite him up to go over a little business deal. One of the security people comes by to tell me someone's at the front desk asking for me.

"I make my way through the office to the entry foyer, where I spot a familiar face. He's in a rumpled baseball jacket, hiking boots, string tie. 'Jim?,' he says. 'Jim, issat you, old buddy? Almost didn't recognize you without a spinning rod,' " reports James Gregory Leiting, a Boston electronics entrepreneur.

"Old flannel shirts, beat-up hats, patches on your jeans—it's what everybody wore out on the boats. It seems it was also what he wore off the boats. I felt a little embarrassed. Not for me, mind you. For him—security refused to let him in. I thought to myself, someone needs to tell him to get with the program. But I didn't want to be the one."

By dressing the way he did, Jim's friend put unspoken but nevertheless real limits on the relationship between them. It made Jim wonder about his pal's judgment. If he had been Jim's employee, the career consequences could have been serious. As it was, from then on Jim kept in contact with his fishing buddy strictly via telephone.

My personal take on Jim's story is this: There is no one correct way to dress and look that works everywhere. Tailored clothes in a fishing camp are as out of place as the lack of them in tonier settings.

Whether the way you dress in any given situation creates a positive impression or a negative one, your appearance counts. Nobody is neutral about the way we present ourselves. Directly or indirectly, this affects how they behave toward you, whether they trust you, and how they think you will behave.

TO GET THE PART, DRESS THE PART

"I used to get annoyed about being judged by my wardrobe until my mentor asked me to imagine I had a million dollars to invest. She said I was interviewing three people to handle my money and make it grow. It was up to me to choose one of them," reports Cincinnati corporate worker Dale Dunne. "The first wears a well-tailored, dark blue suit. The second, a khaki bush coat, a silk shirt in a neat pattern, designer jeans, and English riding boots. The third is a Hell's Angel in a leather get-up. Next, she asked me to imagine the same three people dressed the same ways, only now I am interested first in learning how to run and repair motorcycles, and second, buying some pedigreed puppies. I got her point."

Dale's three examples may seem extreme. But the lesson they deliver makes solid sense. We immediately size up people based on their appearance. We attribute certain qualities—favorable or unfavorable—based on our expectations and the way they are dressed for the situation. We make choices about how to behave towards them accordingly.

Appearance, in other words, counts—even to people who once thought it unfair to judge others by the clothes they wear.

Like every other aspect of human relations, the way you dress has both to please you and the people with whom you come in contact—at least to the extent that what you wear does not put them off. This is not to argue for a one-look-fits-all approach to wardrobe. Rather, it is to say that dress inappropriate to the circumstance produces more confusion than confidence. It makes your personal journey to a corner office a whole lot harder than it has to be—perhaps even impossible.

℞2: Forget fashion; dress smart.

"The clothing industry and fashion magazines are in the business of separating people from money," reports Kelly Kerwick, a former high-fashion model who now writes a regular column for one of the consumer magazines, from her home base in California's Napa Valley.

"They design and promote new clothes for just one reason. To replace the new clothes you bought last year."

Kelly's insight sheds light on the point I want to make: It is always more in your interest—economic and career—to dress smart than to dress in fashion.

What do I mean by *smart*? I mean that, man or woman, young or old, you must dress in a way that means business not to the editors of *Gentlemen's Quarterly* and *Vogue*, most of whom have never known the challenge of an operating job. No, your clothes must mean business to a far more formidable audience: the people who run the organization that employs you. And I'll tell you why in the next seven words: They are where you want to be.

Figure it out for yourself. One of the reasons that got them there is the ability to dress the part. Their wardrobe skills have already won senior management's stamp of approval. If that were not the case, they'd never have gotten the promotions they've won. The way they see things, anything radically different from theirs in the way of look raises questions about the ability to fit in and team play.

To succeed, to be invited to sit in higher circles, you must dress in ways that do not violate their norms. This is not to say that to dress smart you must wear what they wear. It does mean you need to take their taste into account. I'll show you how a little further on, in ℞3.

Meanwhile, 25 years of daily contact with corporate head honchos all across America tell me that, as a rule, upper management doesn't put much store by clothing novelty. The exceptions are in the fashion trade itself, show business, retailing, cosmetics, and the like. If this is your lot, you are one of the rare people to whom "fashion" and "smart" are one and the same. The best advice I can offer you is to trade this chapter in for a subscription to a fashion magazine.

For those of you who choose to read on—the vast majority—we can safely be guided by the idea that, unless your upper echelons do, it's really not a good idea to overhaul your basic wardrobe every time lapels grow wider or narrower, or hemlines dance up or down.

HOW TO LOOK THE PART WITHOUT THE DEBT

Your basic wardrobe—coats, suits, separates, and other high-ticket items—should be assembled for the long pull (about which I'll have more to say in ℞12).

Accessories, on the other hand—blouses and shirts and sweaters, neckwear, footwear, hosiery, and so on—are your fashion consumables. Careful and timely selection of these add a contemporary touch to your basic look and refresh daily the image your wardrobe presents.

I don't care if your organization is charitable or for-profit, in manufacturing or marketing, national or local, part of government or private, the rule is ironbound: Do not under any business circumstances—never—dress to suit any opinion other than the ones that count: yours and those of the people who run the organization you either work for or want to work for.

Why you must pick your clothes yourself

Be especially sure you never dress for, or are being dressed by, your friend, spouse, significant other . . . you get the picture. To the degree their sense of color or pattern or style resonates with, or is influenced by, what they see in the fashion press, it is not likely to be in tune with the clothing attitudes in your particular workplace.

Dress for, or be dressed by, them in your personal life.

On the job, the target audience is you and the people who run the organization that employs you. Period.

℞3: Stop dressing for the job you have. Start dressing for the job you want.

"The big mistake a lot of people make is to compete for the job they already hold instead of immediately putting on a full court press to win the next rung up the career ladder," reports Walter Grepps, a Houston human-resources counselor. "When jobs are tight there's more competition for each and every promotion. No one's going to push you along just because you satisfy the requirements of your present job description. They want a guarantee that you've got more of what it takes to handle a promotion than the next person. You've got to show them you know how to look and act the part before they'll give it to you."

The value of Walter's advice lies in its simplicity: Dress for where you are going, not where you are at.

THE KEYS TO A WINNING WARDROBE

I want you to have a simple but absolutely failsafe way to determine exactly what your wardrobe needs to be if it is to enhance your chances of promotion in your organization. The basis of my tested and proven approach is to identify a model of the person you wish to become.

1. Your direct boss makes the best model. Barring that, select any same-gender person in your organization doing work you'd like to do at the level you want to do it. The person you choose must be someone who's already got the success you're after. The fact that they hold the job says management believes they belong there, so you can be certain that the way they dress is what it takes.
2. Over a period of two working weeks, use the following worksheet to pay very careful attention to the way your model dresses. To avoid seeming too obvious, make your entries after normal business hours—perhaps at home. Do they wear suits or dress down? What colors do they wear? In what combinations? What about accessories? I've filled in the blanks for Day 1 to give you the idea of what you need to observe.
3. At the end of two working weeks you will have secretly inventoried the contents of your model's closets and drawers from the privacy of your own space.

When your notes are complete, it's time to draw some conclusions about the look your model effects—style, colors, and combinations that add up to your image of the person.

	Clothes	Color	Fabric	Style	Shoes	Other
Day 1	Suit	Blue-grey	Tweed	2-button, natural shoulder	Black wing-tip	Striped tie, white shirt, dark socks
Day 2						
Day 3						
Day 4						
Day 5						
Day 6						
Day 7						
Day 8						
Day 9						
Day 10						

The idea is not to copy the clothes of your model so much as the look their clothes create. For instance, if your model's overall look is tailored, and you prefer close-fitting, it's probably a good idea to save close-fitting for your personal life. Ditto, if you like bold-patterned sports coats and they go for navy-blue blazers. Conclusions like these—the little details that add up to a more general picture—will help guide what you buy and what you wear.

There is more than one way to dress for power and confidence. The art of it is to fit the general template in ways that match your taste and flatter your individuality.

Whether you are a salesperson or a systems engineer, an old hand or a Janey-come-lately, training yourself to dress along the lines of the person you want to be makes becoming what you want to be possible.

℞4: Create a wardrobe plan.

You need more than a wardrobe. You need a wardrobe plan.

A wardrobe plan is an invisible hand that guides your every clothing decision. It takes into account

- The clothes you need
- What you already own
- The amount you need to spend
- When to spend it

We'll take these one at a time.

℞5: Start by creating your basic working wardrobe.

I define a basic working wardrobe as the affordable minimum of clothing and accessories—which are listed below—to give you a different look each day of the week for two solid weeks before a combination repeats itself exactly.

Used wisely, your basic working wardrobe will lead others to admire what they believe to be a much larger investment in clothing than you actually lay out.

The look I recommend in the following chart is one I personally encounter most often in the northeast. Obviously, adjustments have to be made for weather extremes and differing regional lifestyles.

Since your basic suits and separates are in related colors, they, along with your shirts and neckwear, are interchangeable. By rotating through the many and various combinations this lineup affords you, you create a large number of different outfits. For men, wearing a vest or not adds further versatility; for women, the mixes and matches, coupled with simple jewelry and scarves, is enough to cover everything from the most humdrum business discussion to the organization's annual sales meeting.

When you decide to enlarge your basic wardrobe, it makes sense—with one exception—to stay within the basic color family you have chosen. You will not go wrong if you add solid

Men	Women
Three solid-color, year-round-weight, vested business suits: one pinstripe, blue or grey; one medium grey; one navy blue.	Three dresses or matching skirt-and-top outfits in related colors: e.g., one in blue, one in medium grey, one either blue or grey with a small repeating fabric pattern.
Two blazers: one blue, one grey.	Two solid-color or very simply-patterned blazers, one in each of the color families you've selected.
Two pair trousers, one in a solid color that contrasts nicely with a dark blazer, the other in the related color of your choice.	Two skirts, one in each of your related colors.
One classic beige raincoat, preferably single-breasted, with zip-in liner.	One classic raincoat, single-breasted or trench-coat model, with zip-in liner, in beige or black.
Twelve dress shirts: six white, two blue, four quietly striped in colors that either fit or set off your basic color combinations.	Ten blouses in a mix of patterns and shades that work with the related colors you've chosen.
Two pair shoes, preferably black, one lace-up, one slip-on.	Two pair low-heeled pumps, one in black leather, one in color—perhaps with simple grosgrain bow or other quiet fashion touch.
Twelve pair over-the-calf black hose.	Twelve pair hose: six in quiet solids, six in very low-key pattern in shades that work with either of your related color choices.

colors and very conservative patterns. The exception is formal wear, in which case it is always a good idea for men and women to follow the dictates of Henry Ford. He's the person who said you can have any color Model T you want so long as it is black.

As a general rule, buy black formal clothes—tuxedos, long dresses, and the like. Black is always appropriate.

℞6: Take inventory of what you own.

Before spending even so much as a dollar on new clothes, it makes sense to get as much use as you can of the clothes you already own, provided they fit your basic wardrobe plan.

Carefully list the contents of your closets and drawers, noting color and style of each item. Compare your list to the basic wardrobe. The difference represents the clothing you need to purchase.

℞7: Decide how much you need to spend.

Deciding how much to spend on wardrobe takes very little work.

Simply go through your checkbook and charge records to determine how much you spent on clothing and accessories over the last year. Unless none of the clothes you presently own fit in a basic business wardrobe—which is unlikely—do not plan on spending more for clothes this year than last.

HOW TO ALLOCATE YOUR CLOTHING BUDGET

Suits, skirts/slacks, jackets, coats	70 %
Shirts/blouses	7.5
Shoes	7.5
Hosiery, ties, scarves, etc.	15
	100 %

Assume, for the sake of example, you spent $2,000 on clothing last year and you need two suits, one blazer, two skirts/slacks, three shirts, a pair of shoes, and some ties and accessories. Accordingly, you can safely budget as follows:

Suits, skirts/slacks, blazer	$1,400
Shirts/blouses	150
Shoes	150
Ties/accessories	300
Total	$2,000

℞8: Shop at the right time.

To make room for seasonal inventory, clothing retailers run major sales at the ends of the spring and fall seasons. Depending on the store and local business conditions, markdowns range from 25 percent to as much as 50 or 60 percent off. Wise shoppers seeking the greatest value for money buy for the spring and summer in the fall, and for fall and winter in spring. For best selections, shop the day the sale begins.

℞9: Shop as smart as you spend.

"If you think money can't buy happiness," goes the old saying, "you don't know how to shop." The aphorism may sound dumb but it makes a point worth heeding: How you shop is often as important as what you shop for.

Five Ways to Shop Smart

Make a list and stick to it.
Shop alone, especially if you are a man.
Buy basics on a three-year plan.
Shop at stores that exemplify the look you want.
Develop a relationship with salespersons and tailors.

℞10: Never buy on impulse.

Several years ago, a group of well-known national merchants commissioned a study to determine how shoppers shop. The data revealed that people who enter a retail clothing establishment without a plan—mental or written—always spend more than the ones who work from a list. Based on this finding, merchants took to more prominently displaying impulse items—fashion merchandise most people don't necessarily need but nevertheless find too attractive to resist.

"I was walking through one of the big department stores one day and a beautiful bow tie caught my eye. I didn't need it but I just couldn't resist, even though I never wore one before and it cost $30," reports St. Paul businessman Dick Percellius. "When I got it home my wife oohed and ahhed. I wore it to the office twice, got a lot of funny looks and a couple of snide comments, and never wore it again."

When you stop to figure it out, it cost Dick $15 each time he wore the bow tie. Meanwhile, he wears other ties in his collection ten, fifteen, even twenty-five times a year. On a per-use basis this represents a dramatic savings.

The moral is obvious: it doesn't make economic sense to shop for a business wardrobe on impulse. Unless you've got money to burn and closets full of clothes, never go shopping without thinking through what you are shopping for. Make a list—mental or written—and stick to it.

℞11: Shop alone.

It's always a mistake to shop for business clothes with someone of the opposite sex—especially if you are male. Their sincere goal is to see you in clothes that attract attention, evoke a response, heighten your sensuality, and turn on envy—all of which are great if you're headed on vacation or a night on the town.

Your career is entirely another story. It places specific demands on your wardrobe. A working wardrobe needs to—must!—encourage the complete trust of colleagues, the unquestioned acceptance of customers, and the quiet respect of competitors.

"If a fellow comes in with a woman, I know that to make a sale I've got to show them coordinated outfits—suit, a shirt, ties—keyed to the woman's taste and sense of color," reports Englewood, New Jersey clothier Kenneth Frankel. "The sales I make to men who come in alone are never as big, but I often think the clothes they select are more appropriate for the office."

℞12: Buy basics on a three-year plan.

Look for clothes that, in your estimation, will be as good-looking on you in three years as they are now.

Accordingly, if your wardrobe embraces three business suits, you need to plan to replace one suit a year. If you own six suits, you'll need two new ones a year, and so on.

As you shop, bear in mind that it always pays to buy quality over quantity. Quality clothes cost more to begin with but prove less expensive over the long run. It's better to buy better than more:

- You can wear better clothes more often.
- They hold their shape between pressings better.
- They last longer.

These benefits bring your cost-per-wearing way, way down.

Don't be taken in by low-price merchandise. It costs what it does not because it's the best that money can buy but, rather, because it is either stale merchandise that never sold or someone cut a corner by cutting quality.

Always buy the best clothing you can. If this means having to make do with one good suit instead of two bad ones, don't hesitate. The good suit will always show you off better—and that's what counts when it comes to dressing like the person you want to be instead of the person you are.

℞13: Shop in stores that exemplify the look you want.

I do not think it is a good idea to buy your business basics from a catalog. For one thing, you can be sure that, on any given morning, tens of thousands of other people—some, perhaps, in your workplace—will put on what you put on. It's a me-too look that says you lack taste of your own so you play it safe with somebody else's. For another, where do you find affordable tailoring to fit jackets and trousers and coats?

Even if the prices may be higher, it's a good idea to find the store in your area that specializes in creating the look you want. Here, careful alterations are usually included in the price, and salespeople are more likely to steer you right.

"Clothes, shoes, accessories—our job as merchants is to make it impossible for someone who wants to wear our look to make a mistake anywhere along the line," reports Los Angeles specialty-shop owner Harold Soong.

℞14: Develop a relationship with salespeople and tailors.

Once you've located the store that's right for you, make a point of dropping in every now and then. Not to buy but to browse. Introduce yourself to one of the salespeople. Explain your wardrobe plans. Tell them they don't have to try and sell you something every time you walk in the door. You want to become a regular but very selective customer. Ask them to put you on their mailing list for notice of sales.

When you make your first basic wardrobe purchase, ask your salesperson to assign your alteration work to the store's best fitter. When measurements are complete, discreetly take the fitter aside to offer a reasonable tip. Your salesperson will guide you as to what is customary—just ask in advance. If you are satisfied with the work, by all means ask for and reward the person each time you make a purchase requiring alterations.

℞15: Find the hidden values in women's and men's clothing.

Identifiable value in off-the-rack clothing for men is determined less by fashion and label than by materials and tailoring. With women's clothes, it's often just the opposite.

"Price point for price point, women's ready-to-wear is less well-made than men's," reports Washington, D.C. consumer advocate Kesha van Eron. "Women are more prone to follow fashion so they discard clothing after a season or two. Seventh Avenue figures there is no need to build in more value than the market demands."

WHAT TO LOOK FOR WHEN YOU BUY

No matter which side you button your clothes on, the important thing is to get as much as or more than you pay for. To achieve this, you've got to look to material and tailoring for value.

Materials

The first thing to look for in materials is the amount of it sewn into the garment—be it a dress, a suit of dress clothes, or anything in between. You want to be sure there is always enough extra material at each major seam to allow for alteration and hemline changes.

Federal law requires a content label on garments. Most basic items are best made from either wool or wool-and-synthetic blends. The advantages of these are breathability, moisture absorption, shape retention, and in the case of blends, wrinkle resistance.

Cotton and linen wrinkle too easily. Silks usually have too much shine for businesswear basics, but often prove useful in accessory items.

Quality rayons make up into excellent women's wear and men's casual clothing.

Fabric weight importantly affects comfort. Weight is measured in ounces per square-yard of material. Too heavy and the garment will be hot in summer. Too light and you'll freeze come February. Year-round weights run eight to ten ounces.

Tailoring

Most of the things I have to say about tailoring apply to all but the cheapest men's wear. In the case of women's clothes, my tips make sense when you move beyond popular-priced items into better quality.

Before you try a garment on, take a careful look at lapel edges and seams. To avoid puckering, these need to be smoothly sewn.

Next, examine the way the lining is set into the jacket, trousers, or skirt. Is the workmanship neat?

And finally, cast a careful eye on buttonholes. They should be evenly sewn and carefully cut—no frayed edges.

Now try the garment on.

In the case of jackets, the first thing to look for is the way the collar lies. It should be flat against the back of your neck. Any garment that puckers or ripples between your shoulder blades requires the tailoring equivalent of plastic surgery.

Next, scrutinize the shoulders themselves. The shoulders must fit if the jacket is to be worn comfortably.

Pants should fall straight. Think twice about buying trousers when the crease is not centered.

℞16: Use accessories to clarify your look, not clutter it.

"Every time you look at your watch, so does everybody else. If what they see is a lot of bells and whistles and glitter, no matter how appropriately you are dressed they'll think of you as basically very superficial," reports Solange Ranque, a Providence, Rhode Island jewelry designer.

"But they'll more likely come to the opposite conclusion when they see a thin, gold-colored timepiece with a white face and a neat strap."

HOW TO CREATE A "TOTAL" LOOK

I share Solange's words not to argue so much for simple watches as to make a larger point. The accessories you choose—and watches are only one of many items—need to work with the overall look you create, be part of it. Think of it this way: Accessories work best by working quietly in the background.

Ties and scarves

The people who make the rich materials that go into ties and scarves need to thank God every day for evolution. Without it, knights of old would still be the only ones to carry the colors of their lieges and ladies. Darwin would say that the things we knot around our necks and snuggle against our necks and shoulders are their distant but nevertheless direct descendants. And wonderful things they are. Well chosen, they give color to our lives and a lift to our spirits.

The best material for men's neckwear is still all silk. On the other hand, the most exquisite women's scarves seem to be the Italian ones made of the sheerest blends of silk and wool, followed by the all silks.

As in most things having to do with wardrobe, neckwear and scarves in solid colors are the most versatile. Stick with the solids and neat stripes in ties, and florals, tapestries, and small geometrics in scarves. Avoid everything batik, and hand-painted anythings.

Big ones, tiny squares—for women on the way up, you can't have too many scarves in too many sizes. Tie buyers, on the other hand, should be aware that the classic tie measures three-and-one-half inches at its widest.

Gloves, purses, wallets

The intelligent use of leather accessories magnifies the attitude of quiet confidence you present in your dress.

So long as it's leather, solid colored, and consistent with the look you want to create, almost anything goes in gloves, purses, and wallets. Gloves may either match or contrast with your coat. Purses in smooth or woven leather should be large enough to meet your needs.

Shoes

Since every shoe manufacturer makes most styles, base your selection of footwear on fit and comfort. Try both shoes on. The leather should crease where your big toe meets your foot. If you have to force your foot down into the shoe, try a size wider. Low-heel pumps, perhaps with a bow, have a place in every woman's basic footwear wardrobe. As for men's style, wing-tip lace-ups and tassel-tie slip-ons are always in order.

Prescription Recap

To put the finishing touches on the subject of wardrobe, I want you to have a recap of the major points made in this very meaningful chapter.

℞ 1: Appearance always counts.

℞ 2: Forget fashion; dress smart.

℞ 3: Stop dressing for the job you have. Start dressing for the one you want.

℞ 4: You need more than a wardrobe. You need a wardrobe plan.

℞ 5: Start by creating your basic working wardrobe.

℞ 6: Take inventory of what you own.

℞ 7: Decide how much you need to spend.

℞ 8: Shop at the right time.

℞ 9: Shop as smart as you spend.

℞10: Never buy on impulse.

℞11: Shop alone.

℞12: Buy basics on a three-year plan.

℞13: Shop in stores that exemplify the look you want.

℞14: Develop a relationship with salespeople and tailors.

℞15: Find the hidden values in women's and men's clothing.

℞16: Use accessories to clarify your look, not clutter it.

To become the powerful and confident person you wish to be, you must be seen by others as somehow different and better. This calls for skill-based action on two fronts. First, using wardrobe, you must plan the image you present of yourself in ways that encourage others to respond favorably to your ideas and views. Second, you must apply new-found skills, the subject of the next chapter, to reinforce the look you present to the world through body language—facial expression, tone and pace of voice, postures, and gestures.

Eleven Ways to Make Your Power and Confidence Felt Without Saying a Word

There was a time Irene Gunther preferred human banking to dealing with ATM machines. That was before silence replaced other forms of rude human interaction: Nobody says anything in response to your question or statement, people point, or otherwise interact. They simply carry out your request—or even ignore you—with an expressionless face, silently, and never looking at you. Their every action and gesture reveals contempt.

"I used to be able to shout back at rude people, to verbally confront the problem issues, to argue. But now the silence—the cutting off of human contact—leaves me without a response."

One of the ways Irene copes with wordless bank tellers who look past her and never utter a sound in response to questions or situations is to use money machines.

"At least the instructions are polite and they end the transaction with a friendly thank you."

Think about this: It is an acknowledged scientific fact that roughly 70 percent of the meaning of every human interaction—business, personal, social—is conveyed not through words but through nonverbal communication—gestures, movements, facial expressions, and silence.

It is easy to understand the hostile meaning of the silence Irene encountered. But what about the focus of gaze, stance, touch, and so on? My point is this: What you don't know about body language could be costing you seven-tenths of the power and confidence you crave.

Self-Test: How Much Do You Know About Body Language?

I've worked up five body language situations. They're fairly typical of what might happen daily on the job, at home, and out in the community. Please read each one. Then, simply select the interpretation that comes closest to your view.

1. The bank officer says he'll see what he can do about speeding up your mortgage application. As he speaks, he rubs his eye. He looks down toward the floor. Both eyebrows are raised. The corners of his mouth turn down.

   ☐ He means what he says and will do what he can. ☐ He's giving you a polite brush-off.

2. You are interviewing. A job candidate smiles confidently as she walks across the room toward you, one hand crossing her body to fiddle with her watch. You make an instant judgment:

   ☐ She's likely to be self-confident. ☐ She's probably unsure of herself.

3. Through the glass walls of your boss's office, you watch Smithers from inventory-control get a dressing-down. Suddenly, Smithers rises, faces the boss squarely in a wide stance, opens his arms, lifts his palms, and speaks.

   ☐ Smithers is likely to be telling the truth. ☐ The man lies like a rug.

4. You are seated on a bench, comfortably minding your own business. A child about nine years old confronts you. With her hands on her hips, her little chin juts.

☐ The child wishes to make herself appear larger and more threatening so as to encourage you to give her what she wants.

☐ The child may have been separated from her folks and shows defiant gestures and postures to cover up her fear.

5. You are at a crowded party. Across the room you spot a certain someone of the opposite sex. He/she stands near the far wall. You notice crossed legs, feet pointing straight in your direction.

☐ It's an invitation to make eye contact.

☐ It's all just a comfortable stance.

Answers

1. He's giving you a polite brush-off.
2. She's probably unsure of herself.
3. Smithers is likely to be telling the truth.
4. The child wishes to make herself appear larger.
5. It's an invitation to make eye contact.

If even one of your answers proves wrong, you almost certainly want to read on. In the pages ahead you will find my eleven practical prescriptions. These tested, proven methods and techniques are helping people all over the country overcome body-language deficiencies. They are certain to do as much for you.

How You Can Master the Secrets of Body Language

In this chapter you will quickly and easily master the essential skills of nonverbal communication—the secrets of body language—for that extra edge of confidence and power in any personal or work situation.

Along the way, you may be surprised to discover that the key to decoding the language everyone practices but no one utters is a skill you now possess and always have. It's actually in your DNA, part of your genetic makeup, one of the keys to human evolution. But, as part of the power and confidence now dormant within you, it, too, needs a wakeup call.

A DOZEN WAYS BODY LANGUAGE FIGURES IN DAILY LIFE

Popular figures of speech, things you and I often say and always understand, give you an idea of just how large looms nonverbal communication in our lives.

Freeze in terror
Lift an eyebrow in disbelief
Tap our finger in impatience
Slap our foreheads to show forgetfulness
Grit our teeth
Tremble with rage
Stiffen our upper lip
Shrug in indifference
Clasp our bodies in self-protection
Flush with embarrassment
Rub our nose in puzzlement
Wink to convey intimacy

Quick as we are to pick up on and repeat these signals, we also miss a lot. And no wonder. The dozen nonverbals you just read are unequivocal. But the intent of some signals—a certain sidewise glance, or the position of a hand, for instance—is harder to read. The interpretation of these—their meaning and consequence—will become clear to you as you read on.

HOW TO LISTEN WITH YOUR EYES TO GET THE TRUE MESSAGE

People's facial expressions, tone of voice, and postures and gestures give away their truest intentions. Much more human communication takes place through these than through words. Understanding comes to us visually by instinctively picking up on, and transmitting, subtle and often unconscious body movement.

We inherited these instincts from our cave-dwelling ancestors. Before spoken language, before even grunts, the ancients somehow came to understand that nonverbal signals made team hunting more successful than individual efforts. And so the team hunters survived and evolved while the ones less fluent in body language perished.

"When people speak," reports Midwestern College admissions officer Filomena Soro-d'Este, "their words say one thing and their gestures may or may not tell you something else. To get the true message, you've got to listen to what they say with your eyes."

Filomena's point is that when you listen with your eyes you hold the key to controlling one of life's most complex events—a face-to-face encounter with another human being.

This chapter gives you eleven practical prescriptions to help you listen with your eyes and act on what you see. By learning to identify the unspoken signals that more accurately reveal what is really going on than words alone . . . by learning to recognize these when someone uses them on you . . . and by learning to use them to reinforce your own words, you'll gain these important benefits:

1. You'll get more of what you want everywhere you go—at home, in the community, and with friends.
2. The unique power of communication that is yours is certain to bring you the recognition you deserve.

Practical Prescriptions for Using Body Language to Make Yourself Heard

The range of body-language communications is considerable. The most important of these—the ones you are likely to encounter on a daily basis—are covered in my eleven methods and techniques.

℞1: Never draw conclusions from an isolated observation.

"I say something in class. One of my students scratches her head. If I immediately take it to mean she doesn't get what I am talking about, it's possible that I could be dead wrong," reports Harvey Eckerd, who teaches English as a second language in Key West, Florida. "But if a look of bewilderment accompanies the scratching, she is definitely telling me I need to take a little more time with the point I am trying to get across."

The life lesson to be taken from Harvey's experience is that one of the dumbest mistakes you can make is to draw a conclusion based on an isolated body gesture.

THE SYNTAX OF BODY LANGUAGE

Though it seems obvious, body language is a language.

1. Actions are the equivalent of words.
2. Think of gestures as sentences.
3. Postures are paragraphs.

Just as with spoken language, the meaning of any one element of syntax is determined by how it fits in with other elements. For instance, an isolated head-scratching gesture might suggest uncertainty or forgetfulness or lying. It might also mean dandruff or lice. But when scratching is coupled with facial expression, the true message reveals itself clearly.

℞2: Develop whole-body communications to put your message across.

People communicate at various levels and in different ways—all at the same time. For instance, baseball umpires don't simply shout "strike" or "ball" or "out." Strong and easily understood gestures invariably accompany their words. Partly this is to make sure that fans who can't hear the call know what is happening instantly and partly to reinforce the impact of the umpire's unimpeachable words on the player involved.

Along with words themselves, the fullest burden of conversation comes at us in three main ways:

- Facial expression
- Tone and pace of voice
- Postures and gestures

Reading facial expression

"I read the book ten times before I saw the movie. But it wasn't until I watched the close-up of Clark Gable's face when he told Scarlett that he didn't give a damn that I understood that it wasn't just a lot of talk. He really meant it!" reports Mildred Spunge, a shipyard supervisor from Newport News, Virginia.

More than words, more than movement, more than anything you can name, facial expressions tell us what a person is truly feeling.

Your face is seldom expressionless. Its movements communicate a great deal about feelings, emotions, and reactions. Key features are:

1. The position of the lips— smiling?
2. The position of the brow—frowning?
3. The position of the eyebrows—raised or level?

Listening for tone and pace of voice

We think of people who speak in monotones as monotonous, boring, and dull. Ninety-nine times out of a hundred they are. We think of people who fire off twenty-word bursts as livelier and somehow more exciting, exotic people. In the same way, we think of people whose tone of voices rise as surprised, and whose voices drop as more intimate.

Though my examples are admittedly extreme, please understand that I exaggerate the point to make it in the first place: How you speak can be more revealing than what you say.

Interpreting postures, gestures, and actions

"The interview was over when the President of France shuffled through the one or two pieces of paper on his desk as though among them he might have misplaced something awfully large and terribly important," reports TV-news-magazine writer Dick Flobejian. "That's when one of his aides walked over. The President immediately picked up the phone, spun his chair around to face the window. One minute I was reporting history. A heartbeat later, I was history."

The point of this little story is to say that people often rely on nonverbal gestures to get a message across. By simply shuffling papers, the President brought the interview to an end. Other ways to close out the meeting might have been through a frown that expressed dissatisfaction or looking at his wristwatch to communicate time-urgency.

℞3: Pay attention to what's going on, where, and between whom.

The process of decoding body language depends on three things:

1. What takes place
2. Where it goes down
3. Who the parties are

For an accurate interpretation, all three factors must be taken into account. For instance, behaviorists say that when we cover up our bodies we are defending the person within. This may be true generally. But, by itself, the process of covering up is not an unequivocal signal. Take someone at a chilly bus stop with crossed arms and legs, and chin pressed down. They are more likely to be cold than to be defending an inner sensitivity.

HOW TO INTERPRET BODYSPEAK

The words say yes but the body language says no. What's a person to believe? You, me, the world!—everybody sends out two messages at the same time. Words tell you what is on our minds, body language what is in our hearts.

When words and body language are out of synch—for example, one of your workers drums their fingers while agreeing to meet a tough deadline—body language is almost always the trustier barometer of intent. Words can be a mask. Bodies never lie.

℞4: Be aware of the other person's comfort zone.

People need a certain amount of space to feel comfortable in any given situation. Most of us operate in four zones. Although the size of these are largely determined by culture—Japanese tolerate closer contact than Latinos or Americans—three zones can generally be defined.

- The *intimate region,* from 16 to 18 inches, is the only space we will take steps to defend. We reserve it exclusively for the people we feel closest to, and feel violated when others enter it.
- The *private space,* from 1-1/2 feet to about 4 feet, is our comfort zone when speaking with colleagues and acquaintances in a quiet conversation.
- The *social area,* 4 to 12 feet, is the distance most people in our culture feel is appropriate to put between themselves and strangers.
- Anything beyond 12 feet is *public space* to which we lay no claim.

"I hate it when somebody I just meet puts their arms over my shoulder," reports Loreen Dopf, who supervises telephone information operators in the Pensacola, Florida area code. "It feels like they're intruding. I move away."

If your goal is power and confidence, you must give thought to the space you and others occupy. Move in too close and they will be made uncomfortable. Their discomfort shows up in the unconscious movement of themselves or things that belong to them.

WHAT THE WAY WE OCCUPY OUR SPACE SAYS

As we enter, move through, and exit spaces we are both sending and receiving body language.

- The way we move toward or away from others reflects how we feel about what has been or is yet to be said.
- The way we sit—we lean forward to show interest, lean back to put distance between ourselves and what is being said—speaks volumes.
- The way we walk tells others how we feel about ourselves—good, not-so-good, bored, alert, and so on.
- Our posture is relaxed when we are with people of equal or lower status. We suck in our bellies and tense up when we are with people we regard as more powerful or sexually attractive.

℞5: Take control: neatness and sloppiness say a lot.

I want to telegraph a couple of quick stories. Here's the first:

"Sloppy people have sloppy work habits, period! I won't hire a one of them, no sir, I won't," reports Indianapolis fashion retailer Zora Gabor.

And here's the second:

"Man comes to the interview for a sales job wearing a suit?" reports La Jolla, California yacht broker Derek von Nimwegen. "Forget it!"

Even if you feel strongly that people should neither judge nor be judged by their clothing, grooming, and environment, you'd be wise to accept the fact that these powerful nonverbal signals say a lot about you, and imply even more.

Whether you are in business or in something else, the way you look and the way you live and perform in your chosen environment tell the world who you are, what you stand for in life, and what you think of yourself.

Think of it in terms of your own experience: don't you always react to others based on what you see? Of course you do!—And so do they!

"I usually make my first meeting in the person's office so I can get a sense of the person behind the résumé," reports Knoxville outplacement counselor Bruce Wong. "Had one the other day. Person's office is filled with fly-fishing gear. That tells me right off to steer him away from central-city jobs."

To manage some of the most important nonverbal messages you transmit, make sure the way you and your work and personal spaces present themselves is the way you want to be presented. To understand others, look for consistencies between what they say and the signals sent by their hairstyle, jewelry, attire, and personal and office furnishings.

℞6: Watch head moves—yours and the other person's.

Movements of the head are among the most powerful transmitters of human feelings, emotions, and reactions.

HOW TO USE YOUR HEAD TO CONTROL A JOB INTERVIEW

When a job interviewer tilts his/her head toward you, they are showing interest in the last thing you said. By concentrating and developing that point, you gain complete control of the session. But when she/he leans away, they are saying just the opposite. This is the moment to shift gears.

- A jutting chin probably signals defiance, a lowered one thoughtfulness.
- A twitching nose is a good indication of discomfort.
- When somebody cocks their head your way, it can either signal interest in or a question about the last thing you said.
- Nodding in an up-and-down direction—even if the nod is barely discernable—says yes.

- Subtle movement of the head from side to side suggests you are failing to make your point.

℞7: Your eyes talk: Watch what they say.

Shifty eyes, beady eyes, bedroom eyes, the evil eye; eyes weep, twinkle, glower, and mourn. How important are eye signals? Billionaire ship owner Aristotle Onassis was noted for wearing dark glasses when negotiating business deals so his eyes would not reveal his thoughts.

Tests conducted with seasoned poker players show that fewer hands are won by experts when opponents' eyes are blocked from view. Good hands generate rapid but unconscious pupil dilation. Experienced players train themselves to pick up on these. Dark glasses eliminate pupil signals. In the process, they deny the experienced player a slight advantage.

The length of time we hold the gaze of others unconsciously determines the comfort level of a conversation.

- The eyes of liars and people withholding information meet ours less than 30 percent of the time.
- When a person's gaze meets yours for more than two-thirds of the time, they are either issuing a nonverbal challenge or something about you appeals to them.
- People who tilt their heads back to look down their nose at you show disdain.

℞8: Control the nonverbal side of the conversation and the verbal side will take care of itself.

The focus of your gaze determines the extent of control you wield over the conversation. To build rapport, your gaze should meet the other person's about 60 to 70 percent of the time.

HOW TO USE YOUR GAZE TO GET A RAISE

Business people, workers, lawyers, sellers, buyers, bosses, law enforcement personnel, service-industry workers, and anyone else engaged in purposeful activity gets better results when they do not allow their gaze to drop below the level of the other person's eyes. The focus is an imaginary triangle between the other person's eyes and a point just above the bridge of their nose. This gaze is especially useful when you ask for a raise.

HOW TO STOP HARASSMENT DEAD IN ITS TRACKS

When your gaze drops to the triangle between the other person's eyes and mouth, you unwittingly encourage a social atmosphere that works against doing business. When bosses do it with employees of the opposite sex, count it among the earliest signals of potential harassment. The quickest way to stop harassment dead in its tracks is to stop participating in it. Immediately focus your gaze on the triangle between their eyes and a point just above the bridge of their nose—and keep it there.

WHAT A SIDEWAYS GLANCE SAYS

In intimate situations, the focus of gaze drops lower still—between the eyes and the chest.

Safe areas for unlimited gazing in all cultures are above the neck and below the knees. Do be aware that it is more acceptable for superiors to gaze at workers than vice versa.

A sideways glance can have one of several meanings. Combined with a furrowed brow, it signals suspicion or critical thoughts. Teamed with a smile, it conveys amusement, sexual interest, or both.

KNOWING WHERE TO LOOK AND FOR HOW LONG

Slow eye blinking—the eyes are closed for as much as one second at a time—signals boredom, disinterest, or a superior attitude. Rapid eye blinking tells another story: it signals disbelief or outright nonacceptance.

Cultural heritage and industrial tradition both play parts in deciding what's appropriate when it comes to where to look and for how long. African-Americans and Hispanics are reared to avoid the gaze of elders. The white middle class, meanwhile, demands it. Here's a quick example of what can happen when cultures clash on the job.

"Three times this year there was a supervisory opening. Three times I considered her. Three times I had to take heat from my boss for being a closet racist—which I am not—who wouldn't promote a qualified woman of color," reports Eli Alexander, a department head out of Gary, Indiana. "Part of the equation is performance. I gave her an A for that. And the other part is trust. D-minus. The real deal is that it wasn't there. The woman never would look me straight in the eye when she answered a question."

℞9: Watch your hands and arm movements.

Hand and arm movements create situations where very little needs to be said to communicate a lot.

Consider the palm. Open, it communicates honesty, truth, and submission to a higher authority. When we swear an oath, the palm is held up for all to see. Hidden palms (especially when accompanied by negative eye movement) suggest a person is holding back, covering up, or perhaps even lying.

Rubbing your palms together says you expect a benefit. Clenched hands invariably bespeak tension.

HANDSHAKES: THE GRIPPING TRUTH

Contrary to popular opinion, the handshake is not a reliable sign of character.

"I used to think a limp handshake was the trademark of a wimp, but not any more," reports Peter Vincour, a flight instructor based in Boise, Idaho. "One of my student-pilots is an eye surgeon. She said she read all the books about the importance of a firm handshake, but she could not afford to take a chance—she didn't want to risk her profession on a knuckle-cruncher."

Knuckle-crunching, by the way, is a favorite of bullies who are out to prove something, usually at the expense of the person whose hand they traumatize.

When you shake hands with your palm facing upwards, it is a sign you are willing to go along with the other person. Grip somebody else's hand with your palm turned down and you establish an early impression of strength.

IS GETTING A GRIP ON OURSELVES A GOOD IDEA?

People who want to be in control unconsciously fold their arms to get a grip on a hand, wrist, or perhaps their other arm. Whether they clasp their biceps, grip hands behind their back, or adjust the band on their wristwatch, it doesn't much matter. They're all symbolic ways of protecting themselves. The problem is, you may feel comfortable doing them, but their subliminal effect on other people is likely to be something less than you'd wish for or want.

The safest and handiest way to stop a control freak

If you can get the other person to give up their grip on themselves, their need to control diminishes. The next time you are confronted by someone literally and figuratively in the grip of him-herself, do them a favor. Put this quick (for you) and painless (for them) technique to work.

Just hand the person something.

That's right. Hand them a pen, a piece of paper, a dish towel, a nectarine, a work piece—anything. The minute they reach for it, bingo! Their need to control takes a break.

INTERPRETING HAND-HEAD GESTURES

"I know exactly when I stopped getting through," reports job candidate Helen Rales, of Flagstaff, Arizona. "He put his chin in his hands and just sat there looking at me like I was a bump on a log, don't you know."

Helen's right. When your listener's hand supports his head, nine times out of ten he's bored. If this happens to you in an interview situation, you'd be well advised to promptly try another approach.

When someone of the opposite sex touches her/his hair while looking your way or talking with you, the gesture signals interest—especially if there's a tummy-tuck at the same time.

Have you ever wondered what it means when people put their hands to their mouths when they speak? Psychologists point to hand-to-mouth gestures as an indication the person is either trying to cover up something, does not feel fully entitled to say what they are saying, or is lying. The other side of the coin is equally fascinating: When we hear a lie, many of us rub our eyes or ears.

℞10: Watch for foot and leg signals.

"She sat on a banquette in the ship's main lounge, surrounded by guys, but her feet pointed right at me," reports cruise-line passenger William Fordes. "Knowing that gave me the courage to ask her to dance. It was awesome."

In any personal or business conversation between three or more people, the speaker's feet almost always point toward the person whose position they feel most comfortable with. In one-on-one situations, feet pointed in your direction are a sign of acceptance. When feet point away, it's likely to be a case of the body showing where the mind really wants to be.

Crossed legs are generally regarded as signals of isolation—no matter if the legs are crossed in a seated or standing position.

"The thing I watch during our recruiting meetings is the women who sit with arms and legs crossed," reports direct-sales training manager Bill Curlock, of Harrisburg, Pennsylvania. "I try not to spend too much time encouraging them to take on our line because, over the years, my success is better with the ones who don't."

℞11: Always take the most strategic seat.

Where you sit says a lot about who you are and what you want to accomplish.

"I always take the seat that's going to do me the most good," reports utility manager Sharon Vernon, who works in Portland, Maine. "Let's say the boss takes the seat at twelve o'clock. If I want to cooperate, I'll sit at eleven or one o'clock. If I want to show that I am really behind what I say, that I am a willing to take any heat that he might bring up, I sit at six o'clock. I never sit at four o'clock or eight o'clock: It signals that I don't want to interact with him."

STRATEGIC SITTING

So important are Sharon's thoughts on seating, I'd like to summarize them for you in a little chart.

If what you want is	Sit here
Cooperation	11:00 or 1:00
To engage others	6:00
To be left alone	4:00 or 8:00

How to break the bad-seating habit

We are creatures of habit. We take seating arrangements for granted. This means seating in its fullest sense—everything from where the boss sits at a meeting to the favorite chair you like to plunk yourself into every once in a while. Yet behavioral science has shown that where we choose to sit can mean the difference between scoring points and losing ground.

Allow habits to continue exerting control and you'll never command the power and confidence you want. Habitual seats might or might not work in any given situation. It's hit or miss. On the other hand, break the pattern of habit by actively choosing your seat and you make your power and confidence felt without so much as uttering a word. Here's a little exercise that will help.

1. Think about your favorite chair.
2. Ask yourself two questions:

   —Am I getting what I want from others when I sit here?

   —Can I get more satisfaction sitting somewhere else?

Test Your Body Language Comprehension

Between the time you began this chapter and now, a tremendous transfer of information has taken place. At this point, you've got all the book learning you need. The next step is practice. The best way is to simply listen with your eyes wherever you go.

Make it a point to people watch. Size them up from afar. Who they might be. How they might be feeling. What's going on?

To get you started, take a look at five body language situations. After you read each one, give yourself a moment to think about your take on what you've just read.

That's all you have to do. Just think about it. Later, after you've thought about all five, you might want to compare your observations with mine.

1. The scene is a social gathering. An attractive young woman approaches a hunky but mousy man. As she walks, she adjusts the waistline of her skirt. He looks down.
2. The boss throws a reception for the vice president. But you notice that every time your boss tries to get close to the guest of honor, the veep turns his back to stop a drinks waiter or one of the people offering hors d'oeuvres.
3. From a distance, a man and a woman come into eye contact. She takes a deep breath, he runs a hand through his hair.
4. One of your employees has a grievance. As he speaks, he keeps his hands in his pockets. His eyes seem to be blinking a lot. You wonder if he's got a tic you never noticed before.
5. It's a crowded downtown street at midday. With the kind of agility you associate with broken-field running, a man walks rapidly through the crowd. A charity fundraiser approaches and holds out a coin box. He frowns and shoots her a sidewise glance.

Now that you've thought about all five, you may be interested in comparing your observations with my notes.

1. The sexuality she communicates through her look and her moves makes him extremely uncomfortable. Looking down signals his inner desire to get her out of his sight.
2. The vice president is showing great concern for his personal and intimate space. By turning his back he is saying that he will not allow the boss to enter the charmed circle. Moving canapés and beverage glasses is a less direct way of saying the same thing: I will not receive you!
3. Each is, at least for the moment, attracted to the other.
4. I can think of two reasons not to trust this person. First, he kept his hands in his pocket. By hiding his palms from sight, he was signaling either a coverup or an outright lie. Second, rapid eye-blinking suggests discomfort with what he is saying. If I were the boss I'd do a little digging to put his complaint into fuller perspective.
5. By itself, a sidewise glance could mean a couple of things. But the frown confirms things. It says that he is suspicious, hostile, and in a hurry. The fundraiser should back off quickly.

Prescription Recap

In closing out this chapter, here's an instant replay of its key points:

℞ 1: Never draw conclusions from an isolated observation.

℞ 2: Develop whole-body communications to put your message across.

℞ 3: Pay attention to what's going on, where, and between whom.

℞ 4: Be aware of the other person's comfort zone.

℞ 5: Take control: neatness and sloppiness say a lot.

℞ 6: Watch head moves—yours and the other person's.

℞ 7: Your eyes talk: Watch what they say.

℞ 8: Control the nonverbal side of the conversation and the verbal will take care of itself.

℞ 9: Watch your hands and arm movements.

℞10: Watch for foot and leg signals.

℞11: Always take the most strategic seat.

Going for that big business deal, meeting that special somebody, or aiming for a raise—in these and other daily tests of your power and confidence, you are confronted by hundreds of different motions. These can mean anything from "get lost" to "welcome aboard." Understanding the secrets of body language enables you to use these signals to master life's opportunities in a way that makes whatever you want a reality.

PART TWO

REINVENT YOURSELF IN 14 DAYS

The chapters ahead constitute a fourteen-day program to turn your life around. Based on the idea that every problem is an opportunity in disguise, each chapter shows you how to successfully resolve a specific issue you are likely to confront, in ways that build your power and confidence. At the conclusion of each chapter is a daily assignment. When properly carried out, these assignments, which usually can be completed in a matter of minutes, put into practice what you've been learning.

Self Test: Rate Your Ability to Win People Over

Before you embark on fourteen days to power and confidence, it is worth a few moments of your time to get a baseline measurement of power strengths and weaknesses.

Below, I have listed the fourteen subjects of the chapters immediately ahead. Beneath each is a scale from 1 to 10. I want you to read each topic, think about it for a moment. Then, I'd like you to rate your ability in each specific area. Just circle the number that, in your judgment, reflects your level of skill. The lower the number you assign, the weaker your ability in the area. Try to avoid the highest and lowest numbers unless you think an area deserves an extreme mark.

1. Getting others to respect your intelligence.
   Weak *Strong*
   1...2...3...4...5...6...7...8...9...10
2. Making your ideas their ideas.
   Weak *Strong*
   1...2...3...4...5...6...7...8...9...10
3. Making failure an impossibility.
   Weak *Strong*
   1...2...3...4...5...6...7...8...9...10
4. Handling difficult people.
   Weak *Strong*
   1...2...3...4...5...6...7...8...9...10
5. Overcoming a bad situation constructively.
   Weak *Strong*
   1...2...3...4...5...6...7...8...9...10
6. Getting what you want even when you are only half right.
   Weak *Strong*
   1...2...3...4...5...6...7...8...9...10
7. Getting ahead without getting stabbed in the back.
   Weak *Strong*
   1...2...3...4...5...6...7...8...9...10
8. Leveraging office politics to get ahead.
   Weak *Strong*
   1...2...3...4...5...6...7...8...9...10
9. Winning instant acceptance from your peers.
   Weak *Strong*
   1...2...3...4...5...6...7...8...9...10

10. Overcoming a poor reputation.
    Weak *Strong*
    1...2...3...4...5...6...7...8...9...10
11. Getting back on the good side of others when a relationship has been damaged.
    Weak *Strong*
    1...2...3...4...5...6...7...8...9...10
12. Preventing the stress of your job from getting to you.
    Weak *Strong*
    1...2...3...4...5...6...7...8...9...10
13. Enlisting your boss's help to go after your boss's job.
    Weak *Strong*
    1...2...3...4...5...6...7...8...9...10
14. Being the master of change and not its victim.
    Weak *Strong*
    1...2...3...4...5...6...7...8...9...10

WHAT YOUR ANSWERS SAY ABOUT YOU

Now that you have completed the exercise, simply note the area you ranked lowest. Follow this with the next-lowest, and so on until you have completed all fourteen.

What emerges is a profile that ranks your weaknesses and your strengths. Each rating below five represents a soft spot in your ability to win people over. If you will concentrate on these as you move forward, you will immediately and dramatically overcome the weaknesses that are keeping you from getting what you want out of life.

Now let's move on to the fourteen-day challenge so that you can start reaping the rewards of some of the strategies, tools, and prescriptions you've been reading about.

ONE

How to Make People Think Your IQ Is Twenty Points Higher Than It Is

Today's Objective

Boost your confidence, improve your results, and enhance your reputation at home, on the job, and out in the community by capturing the critical content of each and every conversation—face-to-face or on the phone.

SUMMARY

University studies confirm that effective listening is worth as much as twenty IQ points. When you capture the critical content of spoken statements, you assess situations more accurately. You are seen as a person who grasps what is said, who understands, and who considers what others have to say. This leads them to think of you as more intelligent than unskilled listeners. The opportunity to build confidence and personal power lies in establishing your intelligence through effective listening. Your assignment for today is to replace weak listening habits with more empowering ones that make others more respectful of your thinking.

How to Listen to Earn Respect

When people fail to hear and understand each other, the results can be costly. Such simple things as priorities, dates, responsibilities, places, and names are especially easy to confuse. More pressing issues are often subjects of listening error, too. When these are compounded by inattention, careers are impinged, business and personal results may suffer, and your base of personal power erodes.

On the other hand, effective listening produces empowering results. The following example shows this clearly:

Dick Schott, a slow-talking, stammering information systems specialist, is trying to tell Arleen Beagle, his manager, about a potential problem with a computer system their company recently put on-line. Even though Arleen has a jillion things on her mind, she concentrates on Dick's tortuously slow thought process.

Though Dick lumbers, gropes for words, hems and haws, Arleen gets his drift. At first she can't believe a system she approved has a built-in glitch. But as Dick pauses, she realizes he is right. By the time Dick concludes, Arleen has worked up a mental action plan to correct the program. She enlists Dick's help to alert the field organization immediately, before any damage is done.

Later, among his co-workers, Dick praises Arleen for her quick intelligence and purposeful action.

The Four Secrets of Effective Listening

Here are the four field-tested ways Arleen used to be an effective listener:

1. She listened more for ideas than facts.
2. She overcame her emotional filters.
3. She used her spare thinking time to listen to powerful effect.
4. She leveraged silence.

When you make these techniques part of your daily doings, you, like Arleen, cannot fail to establish the two-way communications people respect, admire, and support.

℞1: Listen more for ideas than facts.

People take great pride in being able to say that above all they try to get the facts when they listen. It seems logical to do so. After all, if a person gets all the facts he should understand what is being said to him. But there's a catch: Memorizing facts is almost impossible for most listeners. As one fact is being memorized, the next fact is almost certain to be missed either partially or entirely.

The best listeners remember facts only long enough to understand the ideas that are built from them.

Here are two practical tips to help you listen more for ideas than facts:

1. Focus on facts only long enough to get a handle on the general idea the speaker is trying to get across. For instance, on a personal level, when someone close to you expresses feelings of having been slighted, pay more attention to the impact of the slight than to the litany of details the speaker musters to support his or her point.
2. As the encounter progresses, mentally review and summarize the main ideas completed thus far.

℞2: Get rid of your emotional filters.

Listening is affected by our emotions. Depending on the situation, they make it either hard to hear or altogether too easy.

When we hear complaints, we mentally turn off; when others say things we want to hear, we open up to them in more accepting ways.

Emotions act as listening filters. When we hear something that offends our most deeply rooted notions, we mentally turn to thoughts that support our own feelings on the subject. For instance, if the firm's accountant says, "I've just heard from the IRS," the general manager suddenly breathes harder as he thinks, "Those SOBs, can't they leave us alone?"

Simply hearing the words "Internal Revenue Service" cuts loose emotions that prevent the general manager from listening effectively. In the meanwhile, the accountant may go on to say that there is a chance to save several hundred thousand dollars in taxes this year if the general manager will take a few simple steps. If the accountant presses hard enough, the GM may hear this, but the chances are he won't.

The opposite side of the coin is no more attractive. When emotions make listening too easy, it's usually because we hear something that supports an inner belief or feeling. In a flash, our healthy skepticism fades, mental barriers crumble, and we fail to ask the hard-to-answer questions that lead to more informed decisions.

TWO WAYS TO GET RID OF EMOTIONAL FILTERS

Here are two practical tips to help you deal more effectively with your emotional filters at home, on the job, and out in the community:

1. Withhold evaluation. Listen for all of the points the speaker makes. Judgments and decisions should be reserved until the talker has finished. Then, and only then, review the ideas presented and assess them.
2. Look for ideas that prove you wrong as well as right. It is only human to listen for ideas that prove you right in what

you believe. But if you make up your mind to seek out ideas that might be contrary to your belief as well, you are in less danger of missing what people have to say.

℞3: Use spare thinking time to listen to better effect.

We think much faster than we talk. The average rate of speech is about 125 words per minute. But the thirteen billion cells in our brains drive thoughts at a much, much faster rate. This means that when we listen, we continue to think at high speed while spoken words come to us at what appears to be a crawl. We can listen and still have spare time for thinking.

THREE WAYS TO MAKE GOOD USE OF SPARE THINKING TIME

The use or misuse of spare thinking time determines how well we concentrate on what is being said to us. The whole idea is to use spare thinking time wisely.

1. Think ahead. As you receive ideas (not facts), try to anticipate where the conversation is leading and what conclusions will be drawn from the ideas you've heard so far.
2. Weigh the evidence. Ask yourself three mental questions: Is the evidence valid? Is it complete or has something been omitted? Are the omissions inadvertent or intended to mislead?
3. Seek meaning between the lines. Look for body language—facial expressions, gestures, tone of voice—that add meaning to the spoken words.

℞4: Value silence.

Listeners fail more because they fear and misuse silence than for almost any other reason you can name. Even a few seconds devoid of words can make some people uncomfortable. They have an overwhelming compulsion to break the silence with questions, advice—you name it. These actions prevent the unspoken mood of the conversation from making itself felt in the minds of both the talker and the listener.

TWO WORKABLE WAYS TO INCREASE YOUR COMFORT WITH SILENCE

Silence is a natural part of conversation. It happens more often than you may be aware of. Many of us experience silence as embarrassing. We somehow feel it should not happen. We try with all of our might to fill in the gaps. But silence is not the same as no communication. Silence is a natural but misunderstood form of communication. Unless we are silent, we cannot listen effectively. That is why it is in your interest to learn to value silence.

1. Turn off the sound. Next time you watch TV news, eighty-six the sound—even if it's only for a segment or two. As you watch news reports in silence, imagine the story being delivered. Or, when you are next at a shopping mall, find a seat from which you can people watch. Try to figure out from gestures and postures what's going on between people.
2. Ease your embarrassment. When you hit a lull in conversation, use the silence to ask yourself a couple of questions. First, what's the mood of the silence: Is it friendly or antagonistic, cool or intimate? And second, how will the mood of the silence affect what you want out of this encounter: Will it make it easier or harder to share an idea, thought, or feeling?

TODAY'S ASSIGNMENT

The purpose of today's exercise is to make you aware that there is almost always more to be gotten from a conversation than casual listening allows, and to get you to use the four skills of effective listening in a more deliberate way.

1. Write down the names of all the people with whom you had a conversation today.
2. Mentally examine each conversation in terms of my four points: Did you listen more for ideas than facts, overcome your emotional filters, use spare thinking time to powerful effect, and leverage silence?
3. Come up with a better mental way to handle each negative situation. Do you need to change the way you listen to any one person in particular or people in general? Be sure to focus more on solutions than on problems.

Make Yourself Instantly Visible Through Active Listening

Effective listening isn't passive. It actively tells others they are worth your time, attention, and focus. It reflects a willing orientation to people—the sole source of the personal power you want to be able to establish wherever you go.

Building a skill base in effective listening isn't exactly a cinch. It takes conscious effort. But short of an IQ that's so low it requires you to be watered twice a day, you can be certain that when you do the hard work of listening in a thoughtful and deliberate way, others will see you in new, powerful, and more intelligent terms you may never have experienced before.

How to Get People to Act Like Your Ideas Are Their Ideas

Today's Objective

Maximize your effectiveness at home, and enhance your power and promotability on the job, by telling others what you want, getting it, and in the process, making them like you more for having asked them.

SUMMARY

What you ask others to do, whom you ask, and how effectively you follow up will either maximize your personal and work-related success or prevent you from reaching your full power potential in either arena. Getting people to go all out to achieve what you want means you have to win their willing cooperation. When you develop your ability to translate your thoughts, ideas, and desires into instructions they respond to with enthusiasm, people at home, on the job, and out in the community will act more quickly and with greater effect because they know there is no difference between your interests and theirs. Your assignment for today is to develop and practice the skill of delegating for power—picking the right person, what to say, and when to say it—that delivers the results you need and want.

How to Build and Broaden a Base of Personal Power

One of the hardest aspects of acquiring personal power is to learn how to issue personal and business orders and requests in ways that win instant compliance. Personality is a major factor. Some people are habitually reluctant to relinquish control of anything. They feel that no one else can perform up to their personal standards. Others are at the opposite extreme: They ask too much of others, they make assignments that are inappropriate, or they fail to follow up.

Whatever your tendencies, if you are determined to be successful in your personal and work-related dealings, you must know how to tell people what to do in ways they can accept and act on, ways that encourage them to go all out no matter how daunting the task.

> *"I did some heavy lifting in my first couple of days after the transfer over here. I wanted to get a handle on the work and to learn the capabilities of each man and woman on the team," reports Bart Wempe, a Phoenix manufacturing supervisor.*
>
> *"The idea was to get smart fast so I could decide what I needed to do, what my people were able to do but maybe not picking up on, and who the best person was likely to be for any given assignment that might come up.*
>
> *"This way, a couple of things happen. Each time I pick someone I'm sure he or she is ready and best able to do it—and I don't have to hesitate to tell them why. And second, if they're only ready and able, but not so willing, I am enough on the case to show them in concrete terms exactly how and why it's in their interests to do the job the way I'd do the job myself if I were in their shoes.*

"You know, there's a big difference between people following your instructions because they have to and because they want to. I am all for getting them to want to, and production figures are telling me they don't seem to mind; day for day, production's way above what it was when I got here."

The Dos and Don'ts of Getting Things Done

Here are the four do's and don'ts Bart followed to get his people to more than live up to the organization's goals. He got them to live up to their potential.

1. Do select the person who, in your estimation, is best suited to complete the assignment on time and efficiently. Don't settle for unqualified volunteers.
2. Do present your objectives in terms of their objectives. Don't come on bossy, like managers know it all and everybody else has to do it all.
3. Do stroke egos every step of the way. Don't be rattled by emotional behaviors.
4. Do talk out objections to reach agreement. Don't draw a line in the sand unless it's absolutely necessary.

℞1: Select, don't settle.

Avoid making assignments to unqualified volunteers. At every opportunity—at home or at work—always select the person who, in your estimation, is best suited to the work.

THREE TIPS: WHOM TO ASK FOR WHAT?

The key is knowing your audience.

1. Assess individual strengths and weaknesses. For example, some people's best skills are technical, others' are people-related. While it is possible to be adept at both, most peo-

ple are stronger in one than in the other. Try to pick the ones whose particular strong points match the requirements imposed by your assignment.

2. Relate assignments to available time. If you have a choice of two otherwise equally qualified people, one of whom is working late every night and the other with some spare time, assign it to the one with some time. In situations where there is a difference in qualifications, try to go with the more capable individual.
3. Mentally, follow up. As each assignment you make is completed, take mental note of how well the job was done. On time? On budget? Efficiently? The answers to these add to your understanding of the individuals you are dealing with. This increases your chances of always selecting the right person.

℞2: Present your objectives in terms of their objectives.

Spoken or not, the five most compelling words on everybody's top-ten list are, "What's in it for me?"

That means the simplest and best way to get people to take ownership of assignments you make is to show them how it is in their interest to go along with your thinking.

What makes a person willing to do what you ask of them lies not in your ideas or your language so much as in the feeling of self-importance you feed within them. To give it to them instantly, you need to present your thinking in ways that get them to see that doing what you ask serves their interests, too.

HOW TO MAKE YOUR THOUGHTS INSTANTLY APPEALING TO OTHERS

Speak of what you want in terms of what they want. Don't tell them how you benefit. Tell them how they will gain and what the gain means to them in concrete terms. For instance, "When you take the course in marketing I've recommended, I'll be able to upgrade your job description and get you that raise you've been after."

℞3: Stroke egos every step of the way.

Your requests and directions are more likely to be carried out when they come with honest praise for the individuals they affect. Here are three quick ways to stroke egos when you ask others at home and on the job to do certain things:

1. Tell them where they fit. Let people know what makes their role important to the success of the organization or family. "Without your skill, we'd be limping."
2. Allow your need to show. Explain how much you personally need whatever it is you are asking for: "It is very important to me for the family to go to church together."
3. Express mutual interest. Find a way to get across the idea that you want to be part of their success because they are so much a part of yours.

℞4: Talk out objections to reach agreement.

If policy or family necessity demands that a certain thing be done in a certain way, you have no choice but to draw a line in the sand. Otherwise, try not to unduly insist on having your way. You are more likely to get what you want when the assignment is based on a meeting of the minds: You show respect for the other person when you are willing to come to agreement on what's to be done and when it is due.

The key to coming to agreement with others is to be able to identify and overcome any objections to your instructions that might arise.

TWO QUICK WAYS TO REACH AGREEMENT

1. Discuss the pros and cons. Don't be rattled by an objection, especially if it is emotional. Instead, get the other person to talk about why she/he isn't easily persuaded by your thinking. Discuss the pros and cons. Take the time to answer any

misunderstanding about what you want and why you want it when you do.

2. Ask them to give it a try. Assuming you do not hear anything that changes your mind, ask the other person to give your thinking a try. Be sure to leave the door open for further discussion should that be necessary.

TODAY'S ASSIGNMENT

The purpose of today's exercise is to open an expressway in your mind that leads straight to power. It is based on the conscious application of the four do's and don'ts of getting things done with and through others.

1. Think of all the instructions you have issued in the past week.
2. List the three most difficult situations, ones in which, for personal or work-related reasons, instructions were either difficult to issue or were not carried out properly.
3. Apply my do's and don'ts to each situation: Did you select or did you settle? Did you present your objectives in terms of their objectives? Did you make other people feel good about following your orders? Did you maintain your flexibility by talking over each assignment with the person you chose?
4. Commit not to repeat any of the mistakes you might have made by making mental plans to henceforth handle similar situations in ways that contribute to your base of personal power.

GAIN WILLING COOPERATION BY CREATING COMMON GOALS

Triggering the desire to follow your workplace instructions is a critical leadership skill. It gets people to reach for excellence—to go all out to do or think or be whatever it is you ask of them. In the process of living up to the organization's goals, they live up to their potential—which, in the end, makes your base of power stronger and stronger. Likewise, because people in your personal life understand that what you ask is in some way connected to their personal interests, they, too, will look to you for the leadership you are out to achieve.

How to Make Failure an Impossibility

Today's Objective

Take control! Get the negotiating power you want. Cut through tension, frustration, and confusion in take-charge ways that build strong and enduring relationships grounded in mutual consideration and respect.

SUMMARY

We all need to be heard and respected, to say what we want and feel without jeopardizing the relationships that are the basis of our power and confidence. Whether your role is as parent, boss, co-worker, employee, potential business partner, friend, adversary, new acquaintance, or stranger, the secret of getting what you want lies not in where you express yourself or with whom. More than anything else, *how* you present your thinking determines the feelings of others toward you. The opportunity to enhance your power requires not the ability to argue but the ability to negotiate—to turn indifference to attention, conflict into cooperation, and rejection into acceptance. Your assignment for today is to determine what you genuinely want, and to put your ideas forward in ways that strengthen your relationships and build connections.

Win-Win Negotiating Strategies

Serious consequences in your business and personal life can occur when conversation breaks down or agreement can't be reached. Whether it is with a prospective employer, inside the family, or among friends and acquaintances, it is always to your advantage to be able to work things out in ways that give everybody some of what they want.

Allowing things to deteriorate into an argument sooner or later robs you of the very power and confidence you seek. This is so because an argument has two sides, yours and the other person's. The outcome always produces a loser. Losers never forget. Sooner or later, and probably unconsciously, they take revenge. Meanwhile, because a negotiation has three sides—yours, theirs, and common ground—no one can possibly lose. Simply allowing more than one person to win makes failure—yours or theirs—one hundred percent impossible.

Paul Warres was delighted to find himself telling Marlene Gurns, a free-lance graphic artist, the job was hers.

Marlene, who wanted to design a series of children's books, came to the interview determined to impress Paul, the editor in charge of hiring illustrators. And impress she did! "As much for her willingness to meet our publishing goals but remain true to her artistic values," reports Paul, "as for the strength with which she put these ideas forth."

Paul and the people in his group had put a lot of time into developing the series. Over a period of months they explored the upside and downside of several possible approaches before settling on one that seemed both do-able with the resources at their command, and attractive to book buyers. "When I explained our evaluation, she agreed with many of our decisions, but had strong feelings about how she might approach things differently in several other areas. After we talked these over and came to agreement, I was convinced she was right for the work because she really understands the meaning of give and take."

THREE SECRETS OF SUCCESSFUL NEGOTIATORS

At the heart of Marlene's ability to win Paul over are three questions you, like Marlene, must ask yourself in every negotiating situation:

1. What am I out to get?
2. What are they looking for?
3. Where is common ground?

My hope is that the basic principles these embody, and the time-tested techniques they embrace, will help you reach new levels of understanding and agreement in your work and personal life.

How to Negotiate Successfully

Here are three deceptively simple but highly effective secrets of negotiating success—the ones that turn distance into attention, conflict into cooperation, and dreams into realities.

℞1: Know what you want.

Here's a quick and time-tested technique to help you decide what you really want.

EXAMINE YOUR OPTIONS

Give yourself five minutes to daydream. Think about a particular situation and all of the things you might want out of it. Try to make each option you think up as specific as you can: not "make more money," but, rather, "make a six-figure income." Write each one down as it occurs. Later, read your list over. Get your head cranking about what you've written. Think up still more options. Keep on doing this until you run out of ideas. Go over the list once more; throw out weak items. You can be sure that what remains is what you want in a given situation. Just decide which one takes top priority.

℞2: Let the words and actions of others tell you what they want.

READ BETWEEN THE LINES

The words people choose reveal some of their most fundamental needs and wants. Here are three quick listening tips followed by three tips on how to interpret what is being said between the lines:

Listening tips

1. Make direct listening contact with what they are saying, not what you want them to say or are afraid they will say.
2. Don't filter their words through your emotions. It is counterproductive to listen for words that tweak your worst fears. What you fear most is unlikely to happen.
3. Stop looking for hints that suggest you are less powerful than the other person. You have enough power. All you need to do is wake it up.

Interpreting tips

1. When you actually hear words like *affection, desirable, friend, cherish,* or *adore,* they are probably expressing a desire for

closer contact. Presenting your thought in terms of its personal impact on them is your best approach.

2. When people use words like *annoyed, put out, frustrated, furious,* or *violent,* they are telling you one of the things they want is for your thoughts to come across in a calm and calming manner.
3. Words that signal confusion and uncertainty in their minds include *undecided, vague, baffled, mixed up, foggy, lost,* and *muddled.* Inside and deep down, you can bet the farm they are less certain about what they want than their words might suggest.

HOW TO DISCOVER IF WHAT PEOPLE SAY IS WHAT THEY THINK

While words can deceive, body language never lies. When what others say they want doesn't jibe with the nonverbal signals they are sending, put more credence in the body language. It's the truer barometer of what's going on.

The quickest and best way to spot truth is to *look for incongruity.* For example, when you are striking up a conversation with someone of the opposite sex for the first time, and they seem friendly but clasp one arm to the other, they are likely to be showing a need for protection—perhaps from you or your idea. What they want is a feeling of safety. Accordingly, your best body-language response is to smile as you speak in a kindly tone of voice, tilt your head ever so slightly in their direction with your arms relaxed and palms facing them.

℞3: Find common ground.

Leveraging attitude to arrive at common ground is a three-step process.

Step one: Speak first to the needs of others.

When you start out talking about what you want, the only person with a stake in what you are saying is you. But when you put their case first, both sides are immediately drawn together.

Step two: Bridge the gap.

Think of a negotiation as two banks of a river, between which lies an island. Your job is to build two bridges. One between your side and the island, and a second between the island and their side. Use the bridge-building technique. It's quick. It's practical. And nine times out of ten it is going to work.

Step three: Make certain everyone knows what success means to them.

The biggest reason people quit negotiations is that they lose sight of the benefits that come with agreement. It serves you well, therefore, to keep the other side interested every step of the way. It works under even the toughest personal and business conditions.

Making certain others know what's in it for them to come to agreement increases your chances of achieving it—even against powerful personal odds.

TODAY'S ASSIGNMENT

To prevent your history from becoming your destiny, you need to learn from your mistakes.

1. Think of the last big conflict you experienced—one whose outcome leads you to think you came out on the short end of the stick.
2. On a blank piece of paper, write down the outcome you would have preferred.
3. Imagine how your preferred outcome might have happened if you knew what you wanted, what they wanted, and where common ground lay. List these things. Try to remember thinking about them the next time you find yourself in a potential win-lose situation.

You Win When Everyone Wins

When everyone wins, nobody loses. From frustrating to fulfilling, from dead-end to exciting—learning to negotiate instead of argue will dramatically turn your personal and professional life around. Watch in amazement as everybody comes away from a negotiation with you feeling like a winner—that they were heard, that they were understood, and that their needs are going to be met.

How to Deal With Difficult People

Today's Objective

Discover the secret inner forces that drive others to think and act in difficult ways, and use the power of your new-found knowledge to make good things happen in your career, home life, and out in the community.

SUMMARY

Difficult people come in both genders, all colors, and every size imaginable. They live and work everywhere. You may try to avoid them as much as you can, but sooner or later you've got to be able to deal with them if you want others to regard you as a leader. When you are able to understand what makes difficult people difficult, the lives of those with whom you interact are certain to be enriched, and others will see you as a wellspring of confidence. This empowers you to solve problems in ways that support the best interests of all concerned. Your assignment for today is to become aware of the ways in which you attempt to deal with difficult people, and to replace these with better techniques.

THE SECRET FORCES THAT MAKE DIFFICULT PEOPLE DIFFICULT

Difficult people respond badly to logic and confrontation. Often, these approaches produce idiosyncratic responses: They become mulish, turn off, withdraw, fight back, grow embittered. On the other hand, when you understand the secret inner forces that drive others to think and act in difficult ways, you've got the leverage you need, the power to make good things happen at home and on the job.

Joe and Joy first got together as founding partners of a mail-order business. Their marriage partnership came a little later. The business prospered; sadly, their marriage didn't. After a difficult but civilized divorce, they agreed to go on with the company because they had worked so hard to bring it along. It was on the brink of national success, too soon to sell out.

Things went reasonably well thanks to Joe's smart buying and Joy's powerful merchandising. Orders and catalog requests grew steadily. But Joe was making longer and longer buying excursions. Joy understood the difficulty: The divorce cost Joe his pride and self-confidence; he was using the buying trips to show Joy he was in charge of his own life. This put so much of an extra load on Joy she hired several new people. One morning after a meeting with the accountant, she told Joe she was concerned about rising payroll costs.

Joe fussed until she reminded him that the whole idea of operating the business was to build it up. "If you are willing to settle for about half of what this business is worth, the accountant says he'd contact the big catalog houses. On the other hand, if we can find a way to go on building, he thinks we'll eventually command a premium price. He suggests that we cut costs by making more of your contacts through video-conferencing. With a good international overnight delivery service, you'll have samples in your hands on a daily basis. You'll still be making all the buying decisions, but with a lower cost structure we can both look forward to getting a price that rewards all the work we've put in."

Three Prescriptions for Handling Difficult People

Joy used three practical, time-tested methods to handle the pride that drove her ex-husband's difficult behavior. No matter what kind of difficulty others present—hot-headed, attention-seeking, isolated, complaining, sarcastic, haughty, fearful, nagging, teasing, shouting, obsessed with detail—these give you immediate control of the situation.

1. Identify the motivating need.
2. Examine emotions.
3. Relate your needs to theirs.

Whether you are a supervisor or a manager, an engineer or a word processor, a mental health worker or a janitor, laborer, attorney, physician, garage mechanic, or minister, this three-step approach will empower you to quickly, easily, and successfully deal with anybody out to give you a hard time.

℞1: Identify the motivating need.

When it comes to handling difficult people, the very first thing you must do is get a handle on what they really want to achieve through their difficult behavior.

The whole idea is for you to help them get whatever it is they really want. Once you do, the basis for any difficulty evaporates, and things between you can get on a more even keel. Step-by-step, here's what I mean:

1. A baby fusses.
2. Its behavior is intended to get Mom to pay attention.

3. Mom does.
4. The problem goes away.

The task is to find a way to figure out the secret motivators that drive people to behave in hard-to-take ways. Then, when you understand why they are being difficult, you can use that information to guide the encounter toward whatever it is that you want.

SIX QUICK WAYS TO NEUTRALIZE DIFFICULTY

It is an acknowledged fact that everything people say and do is intended to satisfy their most pressing inner need of the moment. That being the case, it is fair to say that each patch of difficult behavior reflects the underlying need that drives it. Identify it, satisfy it, and you defuse the situation instantly. Here are six quick ways to handle difficult people effectively:

1. If they show off, admire something.
2. If pride is hurt, find a sincere way to make them feel good.
3. If they act out of control, find something on which you can calmly and easily agree.
4. If they are protecting themselves from a threat, real or imagined, do not force a confrontation with reality.
5. If they feel unrecognized, pay them a compliment or offer a reward.
6. If they feel like an outsider, invite them in.

HOW TO FIND OUT WHAT MAKES PEOPLE TICK

Getting other people to talk about themselves adds depth to your understanding of their inner workings. The subjects they choose, the words they use, their body language—these open windows on what is really going on inside.

The quickest and surest way to get others talking is to ask questions that cannot be answered with a fact or a simple yes or no. Here are five examples:

1. I'm new on the job. Who's who around here?
2. What's the story on the long delivery time?
3. What signs do you look for to tell you the buyer is ready to place an order?
4. When it happened, how did you feel about it?
5. Why do you suppose your brother hit you?

Listening Tips

It's important to listen carefully to their answers. Here are two methods:

1. Concentrate one hundred percent on the other person. Focus on what they say, not what you think in response to what they are saying.
2. Be alert to the underlying feelings their words and actions convey. If someone speaks in calm words but wags a finger at you as they do, be on the lookout for a seam of smoldering anger burning deep in their personal geology. If their conversation includes words like *worried, on edge,* or *terrified,* fear is more likely the motivator.

℞2: Examine emotions.

Emotions like anger, guilt, shame, envy, and fear breed inner tension. Since tension is unpleasant, some people release the pressure by acting difficult. That's why a wall of resentment suddenly shuts you off from someone you love . . . or you find yourself in a business argument in which neither party hears the other . . . or your daughter, for no apparent reason, sheds tears . . . or a friend shouts and blusters.

ELEVEN DIFFICULT BEHAVIORS AND THE EMOTIONS THAT DRIVE THEM

When it comes to emotions, things are not always what they seem to be. The phenomenon is called displacement. People displace emotions—cover fear, for instance, with anger—for the same reason a magician makes a diverting gesture. It's to draw your attention away from what is really going on.

Driving Emotion	Behavior
Anger	Argument Gossip Destructive criticism Teasing Lack of cooperation
Guilt	Confessions of real or imagined misdeeds Self-criticism Acts of atonement
Anxiety	Overcautious behavior Secretiveness Withdrawal

℞3: Relate your needs to the other person's needs.

Once you have discovered the hidden need that drives their difficult behavior, you must leverage the knowledge by showing them how an aspect of your thinking satisfies their need. Speak of what you want in terms of what they really want.

One of the best and most effective ways to relate your interests to theirs is to open with a general understanding of the need you perceive, followed by a specific aspect of your thinking that fulfills that need.

Here are sample openings you can use as they are or modified to meet your situation:

- "Let me see if this is your situation . . ."
- "It's my understanding that . . ."

- "I know you've got a problem with . . ."
- "What most people want out of situations like this is . . ."
- "Let's verbally outline where things stand . . ."
- "There is always a problem when . . ."

Here are a few examples of how to show exactly where your idea fits in the context of their need:

- "In a situation like ours, *X* is the solution because it works two ways."
- "You get the best of both when . . ."
- "In other words, you are looking for . . ."
- "Here's how my thinking about *X* ties into yours . . ."
- "What we both seem to want is *X*."

Today's Assignment

1. Write down all the difficult situations you experienced in the past ten days.
2. Opposite each one, list the steps you took to defuse each interaction.
3. Come up with a better way to handle each negative encounter. Perhaps you need to put more personal emphasis on understanding what a difficult person wants, or the emotional forces that drive difficulty, or on relating your needs to the needs of others.
4. Today, at every opportunity, replace old patterns of handling difficulty with more positive and effective methods.

Difficult No More

The number one reason people fail to deal effectively with a difficult person is that they do not understand what drives a person to be difficult in the first place. If they did, they'd never attempt the strong arguments, forceful gestures, or emphatic tones of voice that bring them failure after failure.

Instead, they'd seek out, identify, and address the underlying cause of the difficulty. The techniques I've given you here are easy to talk about and hard to implement under fire. At first, the process of identifying the motivating need, examining emotions, and relating your needs to theirs will seem awkward. The difficulties you encounter will not disappear immediately. But with time, the process will become automatic and the growing strength of your skills will carry you to solid ground.

How to Come Out of a Bad Situation With More Than You Had Going In

Today's Objective

Use the problems that come up in daily life as a means to build your personal power and enhance the quality of your social, family, and workplace relationships.

SUMMARY

Do you come out on the short end of the stick when confronting a bad situation with an employer, colleague, or loved one? Do you have trouble keeping a work group focused on your priorities or get irritated when things go sour? We try to make the best of bad situations—problems that don't respond to quick and easy answers—but instead of helping things, too often we poison them. If you are out to develop a leadership identity, you must be able to turn bad situations into better ones. Whether it is with people you work with and for, your family, or your neighbors, when you know how to pinpoint the causes and cures of tough issues, you do more than get things back to what they once were: You actually use the problem to develop a better situation. Your assignment for today is to resolve at least one bad situation in a way that makes you feel more empowered.

How to Come Out a Winner

It's bumper-sticker thinking to say that bad things happen to good people. They also happen to the best people—the ones you admire and look up to. The difference is, the best people have a knack for coming out of them better off than they went in. Not because they finesse problems or shift the blame. No, quite the contrary. Because they handle them effectively in the daily course of events and in the process grow ever stronger.

"This has to be the best week in my life," reports Jake Oxnard, a supervisor in packaging and distribution in El Paso, Texas. "I made some big changes and nobody's complaining!

"For a month my new boss was on my case to do something about the production quality my unit was turning out. It meets the minimum standard, but just barely. They brought me in because the last manager was no better than so-so. I guess he passed his shortcomings on to his employees. I tried to get them to improve their output. They came up with a dozen reasons to fudge it.

"So, okay. Enough's enough. They just don't seem to care. I finally decide to make some changes. Ellman Spence has proved himself as far as I am concerned, even if he's only been with the company for 18 months. But before I promote him, I try to look at how this is going to affect the rest of the people, particularly the old-timers. I could call them in and lay down the law, but they'd take it badly. Or, I could tell them I am looking to fill a slot and this is what I want to see before I fill the job. Anyone who wanted a shot at it would know what was expected. If Ellman is best-suited, who could complain?"

No one did.

THREE WAYS TO MAKE A BAD SITUATION BETTER

Here are the three principles Jake used to make the best of a tough situation:

1. He thought things through.
2. He identified the issues behind the issue.
3. He did not act until he had examined his options.

Use them when people don't or won't perform; individuals or groups act up; your leadership isn't accepted as readily as you like at home and on the job; peers show you disrespect; the boss is hard to get along with; loved ones are flirting with alcohol, drugs, or cults. Here's the amazing thing: The more practice you give these time-tested methods, the fewer bad situations you're likely to run into in the future.

PRESCRIPTIONS TO TURN BAD SITUATIONS INTO BETTER ONES

℞1: Think things through.

Shooting from the lip—speaking your mind before your brain is fully engaged—is the human-relations equivalent of Russian roulette. Sometimes it works, but when it doesn't you are dead.

Bad situations don't just happen. They develop over time. Try to remember that rare is the bad situation that demands—or fully responds to—shoot-from-the-lip solutions. It's far better to adequately think things through before speaking than to act hastily.

HOW TO DEFINE THE ISSUES

Thinking things through begins with a clear definition of the problem. Here are two proven ways to state the problem specifically.

1. Identify the source of the problem, not the source of the solution. Find out who's responsible for making the problem happen in the first place, not the person you might put in to clean up the situation.
2. Relate the problem to the larger needs of the family or organization. For example, when people fail to do their assigned house chores, the free time of other family members is penalized. When the marketing department suffers a poor reputation due to a few bad apples, upper management's confidence in the entire team comes into question.

℞2: Identify the issues behind the issue.

There are two reasons for everything: the one people *say* is the real reason, and the real reason itself. Sometimes they are one and the same; more often they are not. The same is true of bad situations. What people tell you is the problem isn't always the bedrock issue.

If there are issues behind the issue—and nine times out of ten there are—you must be able to ferret them out. The quickest and best way to find out what's really going on is to ask, "What else?" In addition to what things appear to mean on the surface, what else could they signify? Mentally list all of the answers you come up with. The ones that resonate longest and strongest in your mind deserve attention and further thought.

℞3: Do not act until you have examined all your options.

Before you decide what to do, it's a good idea to know where you are! You need to get a handle on the range of things that might be causing the situation, and the scope of your choices.

For instance, let's say your boss calls you in to say that she's had two complaints about your unit in the last ten days from Max Guildersleeve. By asking yourself what can you do about the Max problem, you might come up with the following causes:

- Your unit is doing a poor job on work that matters to Max.
- Max doesn't like you.

- You've somehow embarrassed Max, done something that makes him look bad, and this is his revenge.
- Max wants your job.

By developing a range of possibilities, you create your options:

1. If your unit is doing a poor job on work that matters to Max, you can either change work procedures to meet Max's needs, negotiate with Max, or decide there is no way to satisfy Max and seek to have the work he needs transferred to another group.
2. If Max doesn't like you, the situation is unlikely to be resolved by better or more timely work product. In this case, you need to find out why. There may be no real solution you can effect, unless something you do personally offends Max. If this is the case, you can think about making an apology.
3. If you somehow embarrassed Max, you need to sit down privately with him to let him know you understand how and why he might feel offended. Even though the insult was totally unintended, you need to tell Max you can understand why he might see things the way he does, and take steps to prevent it from happening again.
4. If Max is out to get your job, your best option is to forego political infighting and backstabbing and do what your boss wants done better than anybody's ever done it before. In the process, you are certain to find a way to lead your boss to see Max's real intentions.

Today's Assignment

The purpose of today's exercise is to show you that one way personal power begins is with a bad situation resolved in an empowering way.

1. As you go through the normal course of events this day, I want you to make a conscious effort not to shy away from bad situations.
2. When you find yourself faced with tough going, do not let yourself forget that the best outcomes are the ones in which everybody wins. To discover the win-win option, ask yourself three questions: Am I thinking things through? Do I know the issue behind the issue? Am I checking out all my options before I act?
3. This is your only task for today. Fulfill it completely and prove to yourself you have the ability to come out of a bad situation with more than you had going in.

Manage Bad Situations to Come Out a Winner

You can't wish bad situations away, but you can manage them to your benefit. Whether it is at home or on the job, problems come up that do not respond to standard solutions. When you are able to resolve these, your personal power and the esteem in which you are held both grow.

SIX

How to Get Everything You Want Even When You Are Only Half Right

Today's Objective

Deepen and extend your base of personal power at home and on the job by leveraging situations in which you are only half right to get others to give you everything you need.

SUMMARY

Rare is the personal or business situation in which one and only one "truth" obtains. People see things from uniquely personal perspectives. Where you stand in any given encounter often depends on the "truth" you choose to recognize. At best, you end up most of the time being only half right. To gain personal power when you are only half right requires that you act in ways not to establish your unquestioned mastery of the situation but, rather, in ways that empower you to take complete care of everybody's needs. Your assignment for today is to resolve an issue of "truth" in a way that not only delivers the results you want but, at the same time, increases mutual trust.

What to Do When You Are Only Half Right

Even in the closest friendships, families, and work situations, people see truth from uniquely personal perspectives. Trying to imagine a perfect relationship in which everyone agreed on truth all of the time is like trying to imagine there really is a right answer to the question about whether the glass is half full or half empty. Complete agreement on what is true or right cannot be found among people with normal feelings of self-interest. The simple reason is that in most situations, work and personal, more than one truth obtains at any given moment. Where you stand depends on which truth you choose to recognize. No matter which, the best you end up with most of the time is being half right.

When people fail to act on the fact that they can be half right and still get what they want, it's usually because their immediate instinct is either to fight or take flight. Neither option works: Fighting causes people to dig in their heels, cling ever more tightly to truth as they see it. Walking out solves nothing and makes a repeat performance an eventual certainty. On the other hand, when people recognize it is possible to get others to give them what they want even if they are only half right, the results are empowering:

Tonight, it was Linda's turn to buy the flowers and arrange the table. Approaching the dining room with a vase of fragrant freesia, she was stunned to find the dining surface under a mound of crumpled bras, panties, T-shirts, and jeans.

"For crying out loud, Marsha, how many times do I have to ask you not to leave your unfolded wash on the dining room table."

"Me? Who do you think you are, Ms. Clean? What about the dirty Q-Tips® all over the edge of the sink you use to put on eyeshadow. What's with you? Can't you just throw them away, or what?"

Words flew. Tempers flared. What could have easily had an unhappy ending didn't.

"You know, Marsha, you're right. I do leave my eye makeup stuff around. It seems to bother you as much as your laundry bothers me. I'll tell you what. I'll do a better job on the sink and I hope you'll save folding your laundry until after the table is cleared."

"I'll try . . ."

Whether it's with people who work for you, your customers, your kids and family, or folks out in the community, you must be able to resolve issues of truth in ways that not only deliver results but, at the same time, also increase trust. The more trust you establish, the easier it is going to be to develop a climate of cooperation that heads off future conflict before it can take hold. It might mean arriving at a solution that helps your kids manage themselves better. The better they do, the fewer problems you have to face down the line. Or, it might mean selecting a solution that strengthens a worker's sense of responsibility and commitment to the job. A stronger commitment prevents being half right from escalating to full-scale warfare.

Three Prescriptions for Getting What You Want

Here are three powerful and practical step-by-step prescriptions. These help you understand how your gripes and hopes can safely and usefully co-exist with theirs in a way that takes complete care of everybody's needs.

1. Stay put.
2. Treat the other person with respect.
3. Relate your truth to theirs.

Implementing these simple but highly effective methods at every opportunity will sharpen your ability to sense what others want, can accept, and will act on.

℞1: Stay put.

The key to managing the moment is to remain in the moment. Here are a couple of quick ways to help you stay put:

1. Think about what's in it for you. On the job, think about how this moment fits in the picture you have of your career in years to come. Consider the benefits of remaining engaged as opposed to mentally departing the scene. If it's between you and a loved one, try thinking less about the facts at hand and more about the ideals, goals, and life plans that bring and hold you together.
2. Don't make quitting an option. When you feel you are approaching the end of your string, find at least one good reason to give it another try. It is almost always better to continue than to quit. You may have to give a little, but giving some ground is far better than the complete human failure that follows walking out.

℞2: Treat the other person with respect.

If you allow for the possibility that two truths can obtain in any given situation, you have no intelligent basis for showing disrespect for the other person's thinking. By definition, it embraces as much truth as your point of view. You may not like it. You may not entirely agree with it. Still, the other person's truth always deserves your honest respect.

Respect, in the sense I think of it, is more of an attitude than an event. The way people listen, the words they speak, how they look at others, their tone of voice, a certain facial expression—over the course of an encounter these should convey a total picture of respect.

Among the more frustrating human endeavors is trying to get someone you openly disrespect to give you what you want. When you deprive them of the respect they crave, you automatically remove any incentive for mutual success.

The quickest and best way to show respect is to listen until you feel it. Imagine you have told somebody your truth and they are now coming back with theirs. Imagine further that you expose yourself so fully to their truth that you feel the pull of its persuasion, what it might be like to be the other person and say the things they are saying. Feel it, and the rest will take care of itself.

℞3: Relate your truth to theirs.

To become a master in situations in which you are only half right, you've got to convince yourself from the get-go that you've got a problem you need to solve rather than a fight you need to win.

When folks get to arguing about which truth is truer, there is usually some anger and distrust in the air. That makes the number-one priority defusing the emotions that might prevent you from relating your truth to theirs.

The quickest and best way to put out any emotional fire is to get the other person to talk about himself or herself. Emotions provoke inner tension. Tension presses for relief. The best relief is talk. Ventilating is a safe way of burning off emotional heat. The more they ventilate, the less emotional tension presses.

HOW TO CONNECT YOUR TRUTH AND THEIRS

Once emotions recede, you are ready to relate your truth to theirs. Here's a proven two-step way to make the connection:

1. State their truth first. By recognizing their side of things first, you immediately get across the idea that their needs are going to be taken care of. For example, one of your workers, a person to whom you made a promise you failed to keep, is turning out poor production. The first thing you say is this: "I know it bothers you that I didn't get you the overtime I promised, . . ."
2. State your truth next. ". . . but if I tell you that as soon as we're done talking the two of us are going over to the clerk of production to set things up, can we talk about the FDA infractions that have got the bean counters batty?"

Today's Assignment

This day's work is to resolve a longstanding personal issue of truth versus truth. The idea is to do it in a way that not only delivers the results you want but, at the same time, builds the mutual trust that is the true basis of your personal power.

1. Write down several recent situations in which you did not get what you wanted because you were only half right. These can involve family members, your significant other, and people in community or neighborhood life.
2. Look over your notes. Which one of these was or remains the most painful? In the light of what you have learned from this chapter, how would you handle it differently? Make more notes as you think things through.
3. Go to the phone. Call the person or persons involved in your most painful experience. Tell them what you have been working on. If it feels like a battle of half truths is building, remember to hang in, be respectful, and relate your truths to theirs.

It's a giddy feeling to recognize that you can be partly right and still be totally successful in your dealings with others. Pledge yourself to make this feeling part of your daily life by replacing the old ways of handling these situations with the new and more empowering method you learned.

Gain Power By Being Half Right

It's rare to find a life situation in which one and only one truth obtains. Any time a couple of people can see one situation in two different ways—which is the way life goes for most of us most of the time—the best anyone can hope for is to be half right. From reading this chapter, you know this is a powerful position.

Follow my three practical prescriptions: Stay put, treat the other person with respect, and relate your truth to their truth. Rehearse these, make them part of your daily life, and you cannot possibly fail to turn "half right" into "everything you want."

How to Get Ahead Without Getting Stabbed in the Back

Today's Objective

Reinforce the strength of your personal power by gaining the confidence and trust of people you come in contact with daily at home, on the job, or in your social and community life—even if they've once stabbed you in the back.

SUMMARY

Conflict is inevitable, backstabbing—which grows out of a lack of mutual respect—is not. While it is both possible and useful to handle a backstabbing after the knife goes in, it is far better to practice prevention. This involves both earning and showing respect—two skills that, more than most others, determine the amount and extent of the power you enjoy. By applying your best efforts first to prevention and then, only if necessary, to handling an incident, you will quickly and easily resolve things in ways that contribute to your growing personal power and confidence. Your assignment for today is to make an immediate difference in your life.

How to Protect Yourself

It is important to recognize that no matter what appears to prompt it, the true basis of backstabbing is a lack of mutual respect. Yours for them, and theirs for you. The less you each enjoy, the more likely you are to find yourself with an incident on your hands. Equally true is the fact that the more of it you enjoy, the safer you are.

Nick Haldane, print production manager for a Fortune *500 company, was completing his presentation to upper management on the status of the company's annual report.*

"Nick, I'd like some confirmation on the mailing. Have you worked up the specific distribution schedule?"

"Edith Aubrey is handling it. Do you mind if I ask her to join us?"

Nick hadn't briefed Edith before she was called in. He didn't have to. He was confident she'd handle things well. Nick had a lot of respect for Edith's savvy and her honesty—and no fear of getting stabbed in the back.

"I've got my distribution printouts right here," Edith began, "and it begins February . . ."

Later, when she asked Nick if she'd done okay, Nick gave her a gold-foil star he had been saving for just such an occasion.

PREVENTIVE TACTICS

Here are the two preventive tactics Nick employed to create the climate of mutual respect that made backstabbing an impossibility:

1. He earned her respect.
2. He showed his respect.

Prescriptions to Get and Give Respect

When you make giving and getting respect as much a part of your life as breathing, you, like Nick, will enjoy a feeling of confidence in your ability to handle what life delivers.

℞1: Earn the respect of others.

Without respect, there is no mutual confidence, no trust. Earning the respect of others is a gradual process based on your performance over time.

THREE WAYS TO EARN RESPECT

Respect empowers others by recognizing their individuality, self-direction, and their right to self-determination. Here are three surefire ways to create a climate of respect.

1. Deal honestly with others. Be truthful, fair, and responsible.
2. Listen. Show people you have respect for them by paying attention to their ideas, thoughts, and plans.
3. Express appreciation. Others are always far more willing to line up with your thinking when they know you appreciate their effort.

℞2: Give your respect freely.

Respect, in the form of praise, encouragement, and appreciation, nourishes us by enlarging our sense of self-worth and making us feel better about ourselves. The better we feel about ourselves, the better we feel about others. Said another way, respect given is respect gained.

THREE WAYS TO SHOW RESPECT

People who are on the receiving end of respect are more likely to give you what you want when you want it. Here are three proven ways to communicate respect.

1. Greet others by name. Being greeted with a snort or harumph instead of your name says your name—hence your identity—is not important.
2. Pay attention to their concerns. Listen to what people say. Think about what they tell you. How does it affect their life? How does it affect yours?
3. Stand up for their rights as well as your own. More than one truth can obtain. Give their truth the respect you think your truth deserves.

PRESCRIPTIONS FOR HANDLING BACKSTABBING IF IT DOES OCCUR

Although prevention is your best defense against backstabbing, it cannot shield you from irrational behavior. Should such an attempt be made, here are five workable ways to leverage the situation to build your power.

1. Calm down.
2. Explain the consequences of the behavior.
3. Don't allow anger to surface.
4. Be honest about your intentions and responsibilities.
5. Examine your behavior and make prudent changes.

℞3: Calm down.

You're in shock. You've just been stabbed in the back. Your heart pounds. You don't know whether to feel angry or guilty or both. Now's the time to go for a walk, take a coffee break, do whatever you have to not to act in anger.

When your head is clear and your chest no longer feels a size too small for your thumping heart, it's a good idea to meet with the perpetrator. The purpose is to determine what prompted the sneak attack.

Leading questions—ones that cannot be answered with a simple fact or a yes or no—are the best way to elicit information. Here are three quick examples:

1. "Why do you suppose you said the things you said in the meeting?"
2. "Can you tell me how you see the situation?"
3. "Was there a reason you left out the part about interim schedules?"

℞4: Explain the impact of the behavior.

You must explain to the perpetrator the personal disturbance caused by their actions and how it might be handled better. Talk in terms of your legitimate expectation: full and complete support. Describe the consequences of behavior not just on you but on the organization or family.

℞5: Do not allow anger to surface.

Make sure your anger is under control. This doesn't mean you shouldn't be mad. But it should be controlled anger. This is going to be a rough situation and you need a clear mind to handle it. You may be madder than you've ever been, but you've got to take control of yourself before you can take control of the situation.

The simplest and best way to handle a potentially explosive moment like this is calmly make clear that it is not to happen again. How clear you must make it depends on the situation—but don't leave any question about what a repeat performance will bring.

℞6: Be honest about your intentions and responsibilities.

If you've been walking around with a sign on your back that says "Stab Me," it's a good idea to recognize you laid the groundwork for the unsuspected attack by showing disrespect to others. You must also ask yourself if the backstabbing was an isolated incident or part of a continuing problem in your relationship. If it seems to be part of an ongoing campaign, you must first examine your own conscience and behaviors, and then deal with the issues accordingly.

℞7: Examine your behavior and make prudent changes.

If you conclude that your personal style suggests disrespect for others, for the sake of your power and progress you must make changes within yourself. Only you can determine what these may be.

Today's Assignment

I want to finish up this first week of a two-week quest for power and confidence by assigning you the task of making an immediate difference in your own life.

1. Write down the names of all of the people you regularly work with toward whom you have shown disrespect. Next to each name, briefly describe the incident.
2. Review your list. For each incident, try to figure out a way to turn your disrespect into respect.
3. Set out to visit as many people on your list as time permits. In each encounter, casually demonstrate to the other person the specific form of respect you thought up.
4. Make the commitment to yourself to demonstrate respect in every way you can from now on.

By making a difference in your own life through the respect you show others, you will feel the tremendous sense of pride that comes with knowing that you hold yourself to a higher standard.

Respect Is Your Best Shield

Most workplace and social or family situations with a potential for backstabbing can be resolved in ways that work out successfully and contribute to the personal power and confidence you seek.

Being right doesn't count when it comes to preventing an incident. Respect does. I am not talking about blind respect. People have disagreements about how things should run and the direction in which things should move. I am talking about informed respect: praise, not criticism behind the back; suggestions for making things better instead of complaints about what someone may be doing wrong; acceptance, not unwillingness to adapt to new thinking. As you meet challenges, use these techniques to get past stumbling blocks, find new strengths and skills, and bring out the best in yourself.

How to Use Office Politics to Get Ahead

Today's Objective

Extend your power upwards in your organization by getting the exposure to management you need, demonstrating your competence, and establishing your reliability.

SUMMARY

Most people say they are not comfortable with politics, that they don't have the skills or the personality for it. That's because most people don't understand what politicking is really about. They think it's all blowing smoke in the boss's ear, dirty tricks, and behind-the-back tactics. These harmful manipulations may work in weak organizations where managers don't trust each other or decision systems are confused, but not where good human values prevail. If you want to be a person in control of your career, a person with the power to influence others, you must make yourself known as competent and reliable to people up and down the line. You must, in other words, politick. Your assignment today is to develop an action plan to lead superiors to recognize you, peers to be comfortable around you, workers to believe you do a good job, and all concerned to depend on you.

How Politicking Makes Your Competence Come Alive

You don't ever have to like politicking, but you must quickly learn to do it effectively or the sharks you swim with will eat you for lunch.

Politics—which I think of as a means to make competence come alive—is a way of exerting influence over events. Being good at politics means that, to a degree, you can influence others up and down the line to do what you want done. It's not always necessary to be the best manager, but you should be more than merely competent. The whole idea is to capitalize on your skills by connecting with decision-makers in ways that give you plenty of visibility. To them, you become a known commodity whose competence they can rely on and trust.

The grapevine was humming: more downsizing on the way. A year, maybe, two at the outside. Another 6,000 jobs.

The latest whispers left Luis Ortega, a seasoned manager in the manufacturing division, unsettled. He could no longer rely on being the best manager on the team to save his job. He needed people in decision-making positions to know he was the best.

Over the next year or so, after Ortega took already low costs and shaved them closer, he drafted several reports to his boss, who bucked them up the line. When he was part of a managerial task force exploring ways to increase throughput, his superior technical abilities came to the attention of the vice president. And generally, he handled himself, his work, and his people in ways that drew favorable comment.

The day the company confirmed what the rumor mill had earlier ground out, six of his fellow managers were told they were redundant, and Luis Ortega was promoted.

Three Prescriptions for Successful Politicking

Here are the three methods Ortega used to make his dreams come true:

1. He got the exposure he needed.
2. He demonstrated his competence.
3. He established his reliability.

℞1: How to get the exposure you need.

Whether you call it "networking" or "glad-handing," the first requirement is to put yourself where people want to talk with you. This may include going for a drink after work, playing racquetball with colleagues on the weekend, attending company functions, whatever.

TWO WAYS TO GET YOURSELF NOTICED

But simply showing up isn't enough. You've got to engage people in conversation. Think of it as a two-step process.

1. First, express a genuine interest in others. Let's say the person you chat with speaks of his son's problem with calculus, his brother's new car, and his own golf game. This evening, take a moment or two to reflect on what you heard. The next time you speak, express interest about these matters.
2. Then, put yourself into the spotlight. Suppose you are qualified for a better job and want to step up but need to find an opening. You don't want to appear too eager. So you sug-

gest to well-connected friends, "If you hear of a opportunity that sounds right, I hope you will let me know."

Getting the exposure you need is a very good thing, but don't mislead yourself into thinking it's an end in itself. Quite the contrary. It's only the beginning. The next step is to capitalize on the exposure you get for yourself.

℞2: Demonstrate your competence.

To capitalize on the connections you make, you must demonstrate skills and abilities—your competence. It's more than just the way you handle your job. It's the way you handle people, too. Over a period of repeated exposures, you've got to be able to show the people who count that you are good at both.

TWO QUICK WAYS TO ESTABLISH YOUR CREDENTIALS

Establishing credibility among your peers and superiors is not an event, it's an ongoing process. Here are two tested techniques to establish and maintain a steady flow of information to support your interests.

1. Focus more on a steady track record of successes, some small, some large, than on single highlights. Anybody can get lucky once in a while. The thing that marks true competence is consistency. Sure, making the numbers in a bad business climate is news that should be shared, but relate it, if you can, to several of the small successes that, together, made the year's results a reality.
2. Talk more about the successes of your people than your personal achievements. Proudly tell others when one of your people has done an exceptional job, developed a new way to solve an old problem, or finally broken free a small order from a dormant account. Find something, anything, that makes your people look good—and talk it up.

The better you make others look, the more others will come to believe in your competence as a leader.

℞3: Establish your reliability.

When people in your organization and on the outside know you are reliable—that they can trust the truth of your words and that you will do what you say—they are willing to depend on you. The more they depend on you, the more influence you have with them.

HOW TO DEVELOP A REPUTATION FOR RELIABILITY

Organizing yourself to meet deadlines and project due-dates is one good way to develop a reputation for reliability. Here are two more:

1. Offer them a heads-up. Every time you hear news that may affect other managers either positively or negatively, be sure you let them know (assuming, of course, that you are not sworn to secrecy). First, of course, check out the validity of the news. Once you've confirmed it, pass it on immediately. Don't you want to know if something negative is headed your way? Letting others get blindsided by a situation you know about raises questions in their minds about just how much they can count on you in the clutch.
2. Foresee trouble early and warn of it. Whether it is sales, finance, administration or whatever, every operating plan develops hard spots and soft spots. Hard spots are surefire outcomes. Soft spots are underperforming areas or events which can fester and develop into trouble. Do not wait until a pimple of a soft spot grows into a life-threatening abscess before you make your report. Never spring negative surprises that are already beyond control on the people who count on you. The minute you identify a potential weakness, get the news to those whose plans or thinking or commitments may be affected. They may not welcome the news

but they are sure to respect your sense of responsibility for delivering it in a timely fashion.

Today's Assignment

To be sure that the first day of your life as a politician is not your last, this day's commitment is to develop a long-range personal campaign to get superiors to recognize you, peers to be comfortable around you, and workers to believe you do a good job.

1. Write down the names of all the people who directly and indirectly influence the progress of your career. Include your boss's boss but no higher; your direct reports but no lower.
2. Opposite each name, write down one way you might be able to get across to this person the idea of your competence or your reliability.
3. Attach a priority to each name. Your boss should be your top priority.
4. This is your priority hit list—a long-range action plan that tells you exactly what to say, and whom to say it to.

Put your hit list into practice immediately, but do not expect instant results. Determine an appropriate, long-term means to be in contact with each name on the list—memos, direct contacts, telephone calls, lunch. Make a conscious effort to maintain your contacts on a regular basis and you cannot fail to win the recognition you seek.

You Don't Win Influence, You Earn It

Developing influence within an organization is never automatic and always hard to do.

In most places, the people who count most in the organization make decisions on the basis of information from managers they know, trust, and depend on. These managers have influence. If you want to gain power over your destiny, you must be counted among them. Use the three practical prescriptions in this chapter to get the exposure you need, demonstrate your competence, and establish your utter reliability.

How to Win Instant Acceptance From Your Peers

Today's Objective

Establish an instant base of power among your peers.

SUMMARY

Next to your boss and a commitment to do your work the way it is supposed to be done, your highest career priority is to win the acceptance of your peers. They are the ultimate source of any workplace power you enjoy. Their regard brings with it a steady flow of the information you need to head off problems, leverage opportunities, and control situations. The opportunity to grow your power lies in reaching out to your peers in ways that both communicate and attract esteem. Your assignment for today is to identify a particular person and win his or her instant acceptance.

How to Win Acceptance

The critical ingredient in the mix we call personal power is acceptance. No peer willingly grants power to a colleague they don't accept. Conversely, winning the acceptance of your peers allows your power to emerge with and through the efforts of more and more people.

HOW ACCEPTANCE LEADS TO POWER

The acceptance of others is taken for granted by many otherwise intelligent human beings, and regarded as a birthright by several dimmer others. The gist of their argument: If people won't accept me warts and all, won't invite me to be part of their life on the job, who needs them? The counter argument is just two words: *You do*!

Unless you are a hermit, you interact with others all the time. How you interact determines whether or not they accept you. The more acceptance you win, the more power you accrue.

When they extended the invitation to become a permanent member of The Lunch Bunch—a close-knit group of managers who had a reserved table in the cafeteria—Anita Parrish had been on the job less than a month.

She took the good news with a healthy dose of satisfaction. When the caller said everybody admired the quality of the work she was doing, it made her feel like she just got a vote of confidence in her ability to hit the ground running. With all the unknowns of a new job, it wasn't easy to make time to identify the priorities, get around to see people, observe them, work with them—all the while learning, learning, learning.

When the caller talked about cooperation, Anita's first thoughts turned to her mentor—how happy he would be to hear that his willing ear and spoken advice was making a difference in her life.

FOUR SECRETS OF ACCEPTANCE

Here are the proven techniques Anita used to turn distance into acceptance:

1. She identified her priorities.
2. She found a mentor.
3. She made herself visible and available.
4. She cooperated.

Like Anita, you can win the instant acceptance you crave when you make these power-building principles part of everyday life on the job.

PRESCRIPTIONS TO WIN INSTANT ACCEPTANCE

Your peers will closely observe your reaction to them from day one. Your goal is to create an impression that communicates your abilities, attitude, and willingness. Here are five tested ways to deliver the goods.

℞1: Identify your priorities.

When you make everything important, nothing is important. Job One is to get your career priorities straight: what or who is most important to your success on the job. If you are career-minded, these are, in order:

1. Satisfying your boss.
2. Doing the job right.
3. Winning the acceptance of others.

Notice that winning the acceptance of others takes the number three priority. Let me explain why. Topping the list is your boss, the single greatest influence on what you will do and earn next. Without his or her acceptance, your dreams of power will be impossible to realize. You must therefore devote as much of your time, effort, and support as satisfying your boss requires. Second, you must also devote time, attention, and energy to doing your assigned work not merely to the best of your ability but to the way the work should be done. All of that brings us to the task of winning acceptance. The amount of time you should invest in attaining priority number three is all the time you have left after attaining priorities one and two.

℞2: Find a mentor.

It's not easy to feel all alone in a new place. You don't know who to seek in friendship. You worry about your ability to deliver. You worry even more about the demands of the job. You need someone to lean on, someone to praise you when you deserve it, and put you in your place when it's justified, someone who knows the ropes and will help you find your way.

HOW TO FIND A MENTOR

Mentors come in both genders, all sizes, and every color. Here's a two-step method of locating a mentor you want to work with:

1. Observe all the people holding a job you'd like to have five years from now. Ask yourself some questions about each. For instance, do they show good job skills, do they understand the organization, do they have a consistent track record of success? Rank them in order of your preference.
2. Choose the person you admire most. Ask their advice about something. If they are helpful and extend an offer to give future assistance, take them up on it. If the person you admire most is unavailable, seek advice from the second name on your list.

℞3: Make yourself visible and available.

Visibility in the workplace—your physical presence—encourages casual conversation and the exchange of information vital to top performance. The exchanges, in particular, embolden others to accept you.

HOW TO CREATE VISIBILITY

Here are two ways to make yourself more visible:

1. If you are on the production floor, spend as much time as you can in the work area and as little as possible in your office. This communicates your ready availability to hear what others might have to say.
2. If you are an office worker, personally carry a memo a day to someone on the other side of the office. Introduce yourself, make casual conversation, invite the other person to visit you as time permits.

People like to talk about themselves, their kids, hobbies, views on life—you name it! Your visibility encourages them. All you've got to do is be there and listen. Before you know it, acceptance is yours.

℞4: Cooperate.

Cooperation is the one glue that holds everything in organizational life together. It is team play more than anything else that makes remotely possible business or political or economic goals attainable. It is also what makes your power possible. That is why it is in your interest to cooperate with your peers every chance you get.

HOW TO WIN COOPERATION

Here are two ways to win cooperation by giving cooperation:

1. Go out of your way to help a peer facing a deadline. If he or she relies on your group's work for input, do all you can to get it out ASAP. If you've got some temporary excess capability, offer to pick up one or two specific tasks.

2. Use mealtimes to share scuttlebutt. Although you may prefer to eat alone or use the time to catch up, to attain success you need the information that comes only out of the back-and-forth of table talk. Make sure you offer at least as much information as you take.

Today's Assignment

Today's task is a practical one: to start winning immediate acceptance:

1. Think of a person in your organization whose acceptance you wish to win but have not to date. Plan, on paper, the steps you might take to win his or her acceptance.
2. Make notes on how you might make yourself visible, available, and how you might cooperate with the person.
3. Tuck your notes in your top desk drawer. At today's next opportunity, put your notes into action with a phone call or a visit.

The Best Way to Win Acceptance

Being accepted by others, and the personal power this confers, does not happen by magic or by mechanically following the guidelines in a book. Rather, acceptance builds out of risks each person in an encounter takes. You take the risk by starting the conversation. They take the risk by responding. You then make yourself a little more vulnerable, and so does the other person. As you take risks together, acceptance grows and, with it, your certain knowledge that in showing your acceptance of others you earn theirs.

How to Overcome Your Work Unit's Poor Reputation

Today's Objective

Cause a new and exciting base of power to rise up from the ashes of a bad rep.

SUMMARY

Loss of prestige, failure to live up to potential, disturbed workplace relationships, poor quality, an uncomfortable climate . . . a work unit's poor reputation, or the loss of a good one, has a tremendous impact on careers and economic well-being. If you want to be counted among those with the power to maintain a good reputation or rebuild a damaged one, you must empower others with your attitude, define the issues, and deliver more than others expect.

Your assignment for today is to rededicate yourself to your goals through thought and action.

Your Best Defense Against a Poor Reputation in the Workplace

For people and for organizations, reputation is a fragile thing—always hard won and all too easily lost. When a work unit's good name lapses, more than a guilty minority suffer the consequences. The feelings of rejection it quickens spread like a plague. The self-esteem of every person in the unit—the innocent as well as the guilty, the leaders and the led—is tarnished. Allowed to fester, weak self-images are a cancer on productivity and hence a gnawing drain on the personal power of leadership.

While it seems obvious to say, the best defense against a poor reputation is to build a better one.

The word daunt *wasn't in Winston Gerber's vocabulary even though the job gave every indication of being a suicide mission. They brought him in to turn around a unit whose good name had been damaged. His boss-to-be assured him the situation was bad, but nowhere near as bad as it looked to be.*

It proved worse. Not only did the outside world look down on them, they looked down on themselves, too.

Winston talked up the problem with people in his department and with his boss. Then he got in touch with some end-users. They said the unit produced substandard work in the past. As far as they were concerned, they wouldn't take a risk again without a money-back guarantee up front.

The first thing Winston did was to install a zero-defects standard of quality: a hundred-percent inspection of vendor-supplied goods; a hundred-percent inspection of every product coming off the line.

It was not easy to stir a dispirited bunch. They were slow to meet the zero-defect standard. But when they did, a new and more self-confident aura arose among them.

Meanwhile, Winston wrote to customers seeking their comments on the practical value to the end-user of the unit's new standard of excellence. He turned their responses over to his PR department, who put them in a brochure to prospective customers.

As the base of business built, the unit's poor reputation dimmed until it amounted to a forgotten memory.

HOW TO OVERCOME A BAD NAME

Here are the four plot-points Winston employed to chart his unit's course to a better reputation:

1. He maintained a positive attitude.
2. He listened to pinpoint the real issue.
3. His solutions went beyond expectations.
4. He got the news out.

PRESCRIPTIONS FOR REBUILDING A REPUTATION

Less than a handful of factors figure in maintaining or rebuilding an image: mindset, problem solving, persistence, and enthusiasm. Here is one prescription for each.

℞1: Get and keep a positive attitude.

The word *attitude* is shorthand for the particular way you respond to things. Your attitudes are determined entirely by the way you organize your beliefs. Tie them to negatives and bad things are more likely to happen. Conversely, organize them on positive lines and the likelihood of success is enhanced.

HOW TO COME ACROSS AS POSITIVE

Attitudes are never seen. Their existence is inferred from what people do and say. Here are three ways to signal your positive outlook:

1. Make what you say favorable to the listener. By "favorable," I mean attractive rather than repulsive. But don't overdo it.
2. Personalize the message. Find a way, in either words, body language, or both, to tie your interests to the best interests of the other person.
3. Say it as if you believe it. With the tone and intensity of your voice, convince others that you honestly believe in what you say.

℞2: Listen to pinpoint the issue.

Listening to the people who are most affected by your unit's loss of its good name lets you crawl into their minds to see yourself as they see you. In doing this, you move immediately toward full and complete redemption. Here are three ways to listen better:

1. Listen until you feel it. Concentrate intensely on the speaker. At the level of your body as well as your ears, experience the impact of what the other person is saying.
2. Attend to what they say, not what you think in response to what they say. Do not argue, not even mentally. Don't get overly emotional. Don't feel you either have to agree with or counter every negative the other person brings up. You are not engaged in a debate. Your mission is to learn why the unit's reputation is down on one knee. All you've got to do is let others tell you how they see it.
3. Be alert to gestures and other nonverbal communication. Read and use body language. You can feel trusting when the other person's words and nonverbals seem to agree. When they clash, look for inconsistencies.

℞3: Deliver solutions that go beyond expectations.

While you are in the process of reestablishing your unit's standing, you must be willing to spend some effort to enhance the attractiveness of your work in the marketplace. Here are two approaches:

1. Offer to bill regular and former customers only after they accept your work. This will convince those who are wary to give you another try.
2. Try to expand your customer base. This must include both your internal and external customers. Approach people you haven't dealt with before, who may not have preconceived notions about your unit's reputation.

℞4: Get the news out.

When your program to reestablish your unit's image begins to show tangible results, consider an information campaign based on favorable quotes from satisfied customers. Aim it at people who would find your product or service useful if only they knew about it. You don't need a PR department to do it. Here are two channels anybody can tap into:

1. Seize public speaking opportunities. Service clubs, in-house meetings, customer meetings—talk up your turnabout-in-progress every chance you get. To write an effective speech of any length, always put last things first: Open by telling your audience what you want them to remember. Then tell them why they should remember it. Close by reminding them.
2. Launch a letter or memo campaign. Accentuate the positive: Pitch the new you as if there never was an old you. Sales letters that win business open with a strong benefit to the reader, followed by lesser but nevertheless important other benefits. They close with an offer involving saving money or time or both.

Today's Assignment

To close out this, your tenth of fourteen days to power and confidence, your mission is to recognize that, although you have come far, work remains to be done.

1. Write down the names of the five people who loom largest in your career.
2. Next to each name, write one sentence about how this person would describe the attitude you project.
3. Think about the differences in the way you see yourself versus the way others see you. Come up with one good way to get your positive side across to each person. Try to put at least one of your ideas into practice this very day.

How to Rebuild a Damaged Reputation

Most people prefer to work in organizations that enjoy good reputations. They want to be part of the climate of success that encourages them to grow to the limits of their talents and abilities. As this chapter has shown, no matter how good a reputation your unit enjoys, it can always be made better; and no matter how bad, it can always be redeemed.

The keys are to be positive, to attend to what others say, to deliver added value at a competitive cost, and to share with others what you have learned.

How to Get Back on Someone's Good Side After a Relationship Has Been Damaged

Today's Objective

Boost your confidence by turning a bad situation into a better one.

SUMMARY

The most valuable asset we humans possess is the confidence of others with whom we interact in our daily business, personal, and social lives. It is the bedrock of personal power. When, as betimes happens, mutual confidence is compromised, so is personal power. That is why it is so very important to be able to mend the damaged relationship and go on. Your success at getting back on the good side of others after a relationship has been damaged depends entirely on your willingness to act independently of what you suppose other people's opinions and intentions to be, not merely to react, but to see a damaged relationship as both a problem and an opportunity. It's an opportunity in the sense that not only can you re-earn the other person's respect regardless of what has taken place, but you can knit back the relationship in ways that, over time, make it stronger than it was before the break. Your assignment for today is to tap into the power of self-renewal.

How to Safeguard the Most Valuable Asset You Possess

Bad things happen to good relationships for more reasons than you can count. These can lead tempers to flare or people to quietly drift apart or feel hurt, letdown, abandoned, frustrated, or whatever. The important thing is not what causes a business or personal relationship to take a hit. It's what you do about it.

She had come to apologize.

"Just a little late, aren't you!"

Hearing her boss's first direct words since the incident—that was last Tuesday—Jill felt the heat of his sarcasm. It wasn't unexpected, but that didn't make it any easier to take. She had missed a deadline that cost him a dressing down from upper management. According to the grapevine, her boss was not a happy camper.

"I put too much trust in a new supplier. They were late on delivery. I've taken steps to see that won't ever happen again. I lined up three very reliable sources, and split the requirements among them. I waited until now to come see you because I wanted to be able to say that signed purchase orders were issued and my plan is in effect. I've also taken several other concrete steps . . . I could tell you all about them but what I really want to say is that I apologize for letting you down."

Jill and her boss spent about an hour talking. When she left, it was with the feeling that things weren't back to where they once were, but they were on their way.

HOW TO START REBUILDING

Here is the four-part strategy Jill used to start rebuilding her damaged relationship with her boss:

1. She didn't contact the other person right away.
2. She took ownership of the problem and responsibility for solving it.
3. She implemented her top priority before she apologized.
4. She kept the focus on tomorrow.

Four Prescriptions for Rebuilding Relationships

Here is a proven, proactive system of damage control and reconstruction.

℞1: Don't contact the other person . . . yet.

It's only natural for people to be wary of you immediately following an incident. They took you at your word once, and look where it got them. Nothing's had time to change since then, so why should they put any trust in you when you issue an immediate apology? You can't blame them for thinking the *mea culpa* serves your interests more than theirs.

Saying you are sorry before you have prepared the way for an apology is the human relations equivalent of buying a ticket on the Titanic. People need time to recover, to burn off the bitter feelings that get in the way. You need time to analyze what went wrong and the concrete steps you can take to make sure it cannot and will not happen again.

℞2: Take immediate ownership of the problem.

- There is no excuse for bad planning.
- There is no excuse for ineffective safeguards.
- There is no excuse for saying something hurtful no matter how innocently intended.
- There is no excuse for failing to honor a commitment once you have given your word.

- Excuses don't count.
- Promise yourself not to make excuses.

HOW TO TAKE OWNERSHIP

When it's time to take responsibility for the damage, the best means to claim ownership is through a personal understanding of why and how your actions and words made what happened happen—and how and when you intend to set things right.

Here are a couple of quick ways to take immediate ownership of the problem:

1. Do an autopsy. Analyze the situation. To help you identify the core issues, here are some critical questions you must answer in detail: What happened that you did not anticipate? Could some, any, or all of these have been foreseen, minimized or offset? How?
2. Work up a plan. Think of your plan as the tactical answer to the age-old question, What would you do differently if you had it to do all over again? Lay out the details and timing of everything you need to do or think or say to prevent a repeat of the same situation. Put priorities against each detail to identify which you need to do immediately and which can safely allow to develop in the fullness of time.

℞3: Implement your top priorities before you apologize.

Once you understand both the cause and the cure for the situation, you must make sure it never happens again. If you didn't pay enough attention to an RFP from Washington, set up a failsafe way to handle the mail; if you aren't paying enough attention to a certain someone because of job pressures, find a way to take a love break and make a call.

The time to contact the other person is when the changes you are making to prevent a repeat experience are in play. Your best bet is to use the telephone. Speaking first by phone is a lot less loaded than a confrontation at this point.

HOW TO START THE BALL ROLLING

Here are three quick guides you can follow to handle the conversation constructively:

1. Don't make excuses. Remember, you are calling to apologize, not to explain.
2. Make your apology in terms of their feelings. Tell them you are sad, or pained, or whatever about causing them distress. Spell out your understanding in terms they can accept. Tell them their confidence and trust is important to you. After you have told them all of this, . . .
3. Ask for a meeting. Put your request for a get-together in terms of some concrete plans you'd like to get their input on.

℞4: Keep the focus on tomorrow.

At this juncture, the last thing you want to do is dwell on the mistakes that have gone down. Rather, when you meet, your number one goal is to direct the other person's attention away from the past and toward the future.

The best way is to talk about what you've learned from the situation and the concrete steps you have begun to put in motion to prevent a repeat.

"I made three big mistakes. My planning was unrealistic. I didn't exercise enough control. And I didn't warn my boss in advance of trouble.

"When we met, I was already into the second week of an in-house course in project planning. New controls, including a weekly system of progress reports, were in place. I brought one of the reports with me and gave it to him personally.

"He perked up when I handed him the status report. Still, it took a couple of months of steady effort on my part to get him to show renewed trust in me.

"It's funny about the screw-up: It wasn't all for nought. It got me to do some of the things I should have been doing all along. If every-

thing works out, I'll come out with a stronger relationship with my boss than I used to have."

Today's Assignment

The assignment you will carry out today is intended to show you that it is both possible and sensible to open your circle of personal power to include someone whose regard and respect had been lost to you.

1. Think of a recent relationship damaged by something you did or failed to do. Write down all the reasons you can think of for things to have gone sour. Note only the things you did, not what others might have done to make a bad situation worse.
2. Opposite each item on your list of mistakes, write down the antidote—what you can do to prevent making this mistake again.
3. Based on your notes, write a letter today to the person whose regard and respect you have lost. In the letter, be sure to take ownership of the problem and responsibility for solving it.

Even if the target of your letter fails to respond, it's empowering to know that you are doing everything you can to clean your side of the slate.

How to Fix a Broken Bond

Damaged relationships are, in a way, like broken bones: You cannot allow them to fester. Neglect them and they might end up crippling you; treat them with proper care and, all other things being equal, they will knit together in a bond stronger than ever.

It isn't easy and it won't happen overnight. But with today's start, and your continuing enthusiasm, you cannot fail to get back on the good side of others after a relationship has been damaged—and build up your power as you do.

How to Prevent Job Stress from Draining Your Power

Today's Objective

Grow your power by turning stressful situations around. Make them opportunities for success.

SUMMARY

When you allow yourself to go to pieces under pressure, it's not just you who gets worked up. Infecting the people around you—those whom you work with and for—makes a tense situation worse. Everybody's performance suffers, and you rob yourself of the personal power you need to be effective in your career. If you wish to maintain or extend your influence, you must be prepared not merely to take job stresses and strains in stride but to leverage them in ways that make you the stronger and more confident person you dream of becoming.

Your assignment for today is to do just that—figure out a plan to emerge from a stressful situation strong and confident.

How to Turn Job Pressure into Personal Power

There are very few jobs that don't require an ability to work under pressure at least now and then. Stressed-out people, surprise deadlines, angry customers, quotas, a flu epidemic that cripples a work force, a boss who micromanages—sooner or later everybody has to perform under some kind of strain. When you allow yourself and others to go to pieces under pressure, everybody's performance suffers and power drains away.

If you want to command the abiding respect of your superiors, colleagues, and workers, you must be prepared to take job stresses and strains in stride, and leverage them to make yourself a stronger and more confident person.

This was Charlie's first Christmas season running the pick-and-pack operation. Anything that prevented holiday orders from getting out the door in a hurry was going to impact poorly on business, hence on Charlie. He was determined to keep a lid on the situation.

As Christmas drew closer, the pressure built to keep the pipeline open and flowing. Charlie was ready for it. He knew how to keep his cool under fire, his job skills were sharp, and he kept a watchful eye on people for the first signs of stress. They appeared early. Some froze up. One made really dumb mistakes. Others showed short tempers.

Charlie and his people talked out every stressful situation that came up. This didn't stop new problems from surfacing daily, but it prevented the earlier ones from repeating.

"It was learn-and-go for all of us. The better we handled stress, the more team-confidence showed. On the last work day, the 23rd, we moved a day-and-a-half's business in less than six hours. Not bad for a guy with a lot of job stress and no Christmas experience."

HOW TO HANDLE JOB STRESS: YOURS AND THEIRS

With his first Christmas rush behind him, Charlie had more influence than ever. Here are the three proven-under-fire techniques he employed to gain power:

1. He knew how to cope with stress.
2. He honed his job skills.
3. He knew how to detect and handle job stress in others.

FOUR PRESCRIPTIONS FOR HANDLING JOB STRESS

Here are four prescriptions to help you handle stress successfully. They identify the principal reasons job stress gets to people; why having a job stress problem can be better than not having one; three specific ways to examine your response to stress; the power of a positive mindset—how to get it and keep it no matter what's going on; and, step by step, what you can and must do to emerge from a crisis situation with more power than you had going in.

℞1: Know how to cope with stress.

We assume your complete mastery of the job skills your work requires. What you may lack is a coping mechanism to keep you from panicking when the pressure is on.

Job stress comes two ways: repetitive and one-time events. For an example of how to handle a one-shot pressure cooker, see ℞2.

HOW TO PREVENT REPETITIVE JOB STRESS

The hassle of quarterly inventories, the push to meet end-of-the-month quotas—most of the pressure problems you are likely to run into will be repetitive. When you are in one, keep an open mind about what you can do to make the task easier the next time around. Here are seven critical questions you must answer:

1. Are you shooting yourself in the foot? It's only natural to want to do your best to impress your boss. This may be putting undue pressure on you. To avoid this, mentally assign a priority to each task. This assures you of ample time to perform the most needed work.
2. What can I do to prepare for this situation when it comes up again? Knowing certain demands are repetitive gives you some time for do-and-don't planning. For example, don't approve time off for employees when you expect a crunch, but do eliminate nonessential tasks during this period.
3. Are you ahead of the curve or behind it? Do as much of your routine work as you can in advance so that at deadline you are not saddled with time-consuming paperwork. Although you may not be able to complete a report until last-minute information is in hand, in times of stress it's easier to fill in a few blanks than to have to start from scratch.
4. Have you identified where to turn for help, in advance? Some recurring situations can be alleviated by the work of other departments. Try to coordinate with these people beforehand so that they deliver what you need on a timely basis.
5. Can you cut corners without cutting quality? Many tasks are performed in a certain way as a result of habit. Examine these from a fresh point of view. Look for those you can safely eliminate or combine.
6. Is there an easier way to handle the situation? Look for ways to simplify the work. Determine whether parts of the work can be done by other work units.
7. Who is panicking? Some people treat every situation as a crisis. But just because they do doesn't mean you have to respond in like fashion. Identify the people who cave in under stress. Review step by step what's involved in their tasks. Try structuring their environments so that pressure on them is reduced.

℞2: Make sure your work skills are strong enough to handle a crisis.

Here's one of the most difficult tests of your ability to perform under fire: You've been on the job just a short time and your boss comes to you with a two-week assignment and says, "Drop everything. The vice president wants it done in three days."

HOW TO CONTROL UNCERTAINTY

How you react is critical to the way you will be seen from now on by your immediate superior. You must control the uncertainties driven by your emotions and remain calm.

Here's a three-step process to resolve your uncertainty:

1. Determine what needs to be done. Often, when senior managers make crash-project requests, the people under them rush to follow orders without going into specifics of how and what and where and by whom. The work gets done on a best-guess basis, which generally fails to meet upper-management expectations. To cover yourself in a situation like this, ask all the questions you need to fully understand what has to be done. Then give your boss a detailed memo laying out the work you are going to do. If you've gotten it wrong, there will still be time to adjust your plan to meet upper management's request.
2. Identify each task. Build yourself a checklist with due dates for each item. List each and every step to be performed—everything from overtime approval to help from other departments. Put it in memo form. Direct it to your boss with a copy to those supplying outside support. Close by saying that failure to furnish necessary assistance on a timely basis will result in a missed deadline. Ask to be notified immediately if outside support cannot be furnished. If this happens, call it to your boss's attention so adjustments can be made.
3. Stay on top of things all the way. If the task is a high-profile job, you'll be asked for progress reports almost every step of the way. Be prepared to make them by using your check-

list to keep on top of things. When the project is completed on time, give credit to all of the people—in your group and outsiders—whose efforts made success possible. People who feel recognized will be even more willing to chip in next time lightning strikes.

℞3: Control stress in yourself.

I hope you are not among the people who teach themselves to fall apart under pressure as a way of getting out of a tough situation. But even if you are, stay tuned. Here are three quick guides you can safely follow to control the situation:

1. Put the stress on paper. Describe the stress you are feeling. Write at least one sentence describing each of its causes. Think up an antidote for each cause, jotting it down. For instance, if deliveries were late in arriving, your cure might be to require earlier shipment. Tape these notes to the top of your desk or work station. Make a point of looking at them every day. Next crisis, you'll know exactly how to hold on to your cool.
2. Find a mentor. Just talking with someone about the tensions can ease them. Look for a seasoned pro who knows the ropes. Ask them to tell you how they'd handle the stress if they were in your shoes.
3. Do a post-mortem. Right after the next crisis, figure out what you did right and what could have been done better. You may need to tweak some of your antidotes.

℞4: Handle stress when you find it in others.

Here are two steps you can follow to control a stressful situation and get others to be as productive as possible:

1. Talk reality. In conversation, describe the behavior you observe, why you think it has to do with job stress, how to handle it better, and the importance of their contribution to the work unit.

2. Monitor the next stressful situation. Don't rush in to help out. Instead, give the person a chance to cope. Afterwards, talk with the person about what was done right and what needs more effort. If you see an improvement over time, congratulate the other person.

Today's Assignment

Today's work is to do everything you can to handle the next stressful situation in a way that builds your personal power on the job.

1. Identify all the job stresses that came up last week. For instance, impossible deadlines, surprising events, meeting quotas, and so on.
2. For each stress, figure out two steps you can take to manage the situation better.
3. Commit yourself to implementing your two-step solutions daily, beginning today.

Turn Stress into an Opportunity

Having a job stress problem can be better than not having one. The point at which you first recognize that the stresses and strains of your work are getting to you can be a moment of unmatched opportunity. It affords you a reason to examine what you are doing right, what you could be doing better, and opens the way for improvement.

No job is completely free of stress. This chapter has shown you that the strains and tugs of the daily grind can, if used constructively, lead you to become a calmer and better performer others can safely rely on in a crisis.

How to Go After Your Boss's Job and Get Your Boss to Help

Today's Objective

Acquire the power of a leader.

SUMMARY

It is an acknowledged fact of organizational life that the best and, sometimes, the only way to get promoted is to get your boss promoted. That's why, if you are career-minded, your number one job is to build your boss up every chance you get. How you feel about your boss's competence, personality, or way of doing things is your business. What you convey to others isn't. She may waste your time. He may quash your best ideas. So what? It is wrong and wrongheaded to bad-mouth your boss or even to suggest to others you are succeeding despite your boss. One of your most fundamental responsibilities as a subordinate is to make your superior look good. The better your boss looks, the better the chances of making your dreams come true. Your assignment for today is to tap into your boss's capacity for success.

How to Make Your Boss a Partner in Your Progress

No matter what the business climate—expanding or contracting—you have to help your boss get ahead to get ahead yourself. Doing all you can to support the boss's career interest hastens their next promotion. The opening they leave is your best shot at overnight success: You'll hit the ground running. You are already doing a lot of the work on a daily basis. Plus, you've got the people sized up, and you've shown you can make good things happen.

Thanks to some really good advice from an older friend in the organization, Jonas was determined to climb the corporate ladder because of his boss and not despite him.

"Sure I am after your job," he told his boss. "But not at your expense. I figure that with downsizing and all, the only way I am going to get ahead is to step into the opening you leave on your way to a corner office. When you win I win, so what can I do to help you win?"

His boss said Jonas wasn't ready for promotion. He laid out a plan. A handful of things Jonas had to be able to do consistently over a period of time. For nearly a year and a half, Jonas did some heavy lifting.

Late on a Friday afternoon, the boss called him in: "It worked. I got the Cleveland region, and you're getting this district."

HOW TO GET YOUR BOSS ON YOUR SIDE

Jonas took a hard look at the relationship between himself and his superior. He used three core principles to guide his thinking:

1. He started with the right mental attitude.

2. He leveled with the boss and enlisted his help by promising help in return.
3. He demonstrated support by doing a good job.

Prescriptions for Going After Your Boss's Job

What does your boss really want from you? How do you create a partnership in mutual progress? How does your boss rate his or her prospects for promotion, and what can you do about the obstacles that stand in the way? Here are the answers in the form of four prescriptions.

℞1: Develop an attitude of enlightened self-interest.

Enlightened self-interest means exactly what it says. It means getting what you want by helping others get what they want. For instance, when a millionaire gives a seven-figure check to medical research, she is acting out of enlightened self-interest. By giving researchers the funds they need, she gets the tax advantage she wants.

HOW TO HELP YOURSELF BY HELPING OTHERS

Most of your success in working with your boss to get his/her job is going to depend on being able to develop within yourself an attitude of enlightened self-interest.

Here are two quick ways to build the mindset:

1. Think honesty. Do not allow yourself to think there might be anything underhanded or manipulative about working in your boss's interest. From the get-go you are going to be one hundred percent up-front with your superior.
2. Expect success. You can be confident that any superior worth his salt knows this: The best subordinates a smart boss can hope for are the ones who, from the moment they come aboard, stop competing for the job they have and start competing for the one they want.

℞2: Speak of what you want in terms of what the boss wants.

When you think the time is right, seek a meeting with your boss. Your best bet is to wait until your job performance has consistently exceeded expectations over a period not of several weeks but of at least several months.

Talk about your job goals in terms of your boss's prospects. For instance, "The next step for you is to the corporate staff, and I'd like to do everything I can to be your replacement. Now I know it's going to take some time, but for as long as it takes you can count on me for support."

Ask what else you can do. The point here is to work towards an understanding of what you both expect in the way of loyalty from the other. Here's one good way to begin this phase of the dialog: "If you'll give me an idea of the sorts of things the HR people are going to be looking for from our group, I'll make sure they happen whenever and wherever I can."

Your boss in unlikely to turn you down outright, but may give off vibes of distrust. This isn't dancing school, so treat distrust as a challenge. Close the meeting as gracefully as you can. Follow it up with exceptional performance, and build up your boss when you can. A number of such demonstrations may start to turn things around.

℞3: Demonstrate your loyalty.

Being generous with your goodwill—unilaterally, without being asked—costs you nothing. It doesn't in any way weaken your position. Quite the contrary, it strengthens the bond between you and your boss and lays the foundation for the solid progress you both want. Here are five ways to practice what you preach:

1. Work harder than ever. By far the best way to demonstrate your intentions is to do a good job for your boss. Matching your intentions with demonstrable action builds trust and confidence. Let others see you doing what you told your boss you would do. Then do more. People feel *comfortable* with what they perceive to be reliable, and comforted by extra reliability. Be someone your boss and

others can trust absolutely, someone on whom they can rely to do your best and then some.

2. Demonstrate loyalty clearly, but don't overdo it. Make changes in the way you present the results of your work to include your boss quietly but positively in the credit. Avoid overstatement at all costs. Better to say not enough than too much.
3. Speak openly of your goodwill. Verbally acknowledge the respect you feel for your boss and the important part he/she plays in the success of your work unit. Let the people with whom you come in contact on a daily basis know you are appreciative. Use words like, "I really enjoy working with . . ." or "I'd like to take the credit, but if it wasn't for my boss . . ."
4. Use body language to reinforce your words. Back your words about the way he or she handles job responsibilities with appropriate body language: a smile or a positive gesture.
5. Keep in touch. Maintain regular contact, first to be sure the boss sees your competence and dependability, and second, to be among the first to know if something negative is coming your way. Be careful, however, about the amount of time you spend with your boss. You don't want to give the appearance of kissing up.

Today's Assignment

Today's work is to plant some seeds of trust in the mind of your boss.

1. Make a list of five things you can do, without going unduly out of your way, to enhance the reputation of your boss. Try to focus on simple things: a phone call here, a memo there, something you can say, and so on.

2. For the next five days, starting today, perform one of the actions on your list.

CLIMB THE LADDER WITH YOUR BOSS

Working against the interests of your boss kills careers faster than almost anything else you can name. To prevent it, you must learn to seek promotion with and through your boss; my four practical prescriptions show you how. Put these into practice, make them part of daily life on the job, and not only will you get the promotions you want, you'll have the help of your boss every step of the way.

How to Be the Master of Change, Not Its Victim

Today's Objective

Take complete control of your destiny.

SUMMARY

The power to master change is the power to take control of your mindset, emotional life, physical well-being, and career. If you can dream it . . . if you can develop enthusiasm for it . . . if you have the fire-in-the-belly feeling it takes to turn something around on the basis of personal effort . . . then whatever your dream, one thing is for sure: It can and will come true. Your assignment for today is to make it happen.

How to Run Change Instead of Being Run by It

It's not a question of *if* it will happen, for it most certainly will. Change is inevitable. The question is, Who will bring it on? Will you take charge and build personal power through your skillful mastery of change? Or will you sit back and allow yourself to become what you may have often felt yourself to be—its victim?

The only way to take charge of change is to be its agent, to make or motivate change, not wait for it: change that benefits you when and where you want, at a pace you set and can handle, along lines you define and control to favor your personal and career interests.

"There are only four possible ways to change things." Motivational speaker Vern Edwinson's words intrigued his audience.

"You can make small changes in small things but no one would ever know if you didn't tell them.

"You could make big changes in little things . . . but that doesn't get you enough bang for the buck.

"You might make small changes to big things, which creates the illusion of change. That's the problem: it's only a mirage.

"Or, if you are really smart, you locate the lever in leverage by making big changes in big things, . . . big in the sense of being things that are important to you and the people you live and work with.

"In this America of ours, we've got a name for what happens when people make big changes in the big things of their lives. We call it 'success.'"

HOW TO DEVELOP THE POWER YOU SEEK

Here are the four strategic principles anyone interested in acquiring personal power ought to know, practice, and cultivate.

1. Do not settle for what is without thinking first of what could be.
2. Develop a can't-wait state of mind.

3. Make big changes in big things.
4. Be the engine of your own deliverance.

Whether your goal is mental, emotional, physical, or financial, when you implement these strategies—decide what you want, grow eager to make it a reality, find the leverage to make it happen, and take all the steps you can to realize your dreams—you can pretty much count on being the master of your destiny.

Prescriptions for Taking Control of Your Life

Here are four proven and practical ways to get more of what you want out of life.

℞1: Don't settle for what is without thinking first of what could be.

The first step in creating change is to examine the difference between what you've got and what you really want. This reveals two things: First, it automatically sets up the goals you intend to move towards; second, it illuminates what prevents your dreams from coming true.

HOW TO DECIDE WHAT YOU WANT

Here is a powerful three-step process to clarify the question of who you are and what you want out of life:

1. Define yourself as the sum of many parts. None of us is one hundred percent anything. We're all a mix of mental states, emotions, physical realities, financial, and work-related issues. On a blank sheet of paper, specifically define each of your parts—mental, emotional, physical, financial, work-related—in concrete terms. Do not write sentences, just notes. For instance, you might define yourself financially as having a "low five-figure savings account, income of such and such," etc.

2. Identify your satisfactions and dissatisfactions. Think about each part of yourself as you have defined it. Some will satisfy you, others may not. For instance, you might be emotionally satisfied and near financial ruin. Pay no further attention to your areas of satisfaction.
3. Use your dissatisfactions to identify your goals. For each area in which you feel dissatisfied, come up with a specific definition of yourself you'd prefer to be able to write. These new definitions are your goals—what you really want.

℞2: Develop a can't-wait state of mind.

The only way to quickstart change is to surround the need and desire for change with such a sense of urgency you feel compelled to follow through.

HOW TO EXPERIENCE THE BENEFITS OF CHANGE

The way to generate enthusiasm for change is to taste the benefits of the dream. Here's a two-step process:

1. Visualize your goals. Close your eyes for a moment and clear your mind. Try to imagine what life might be like if the changes you now dream of were already in place. Think how much better you'd feel not just in the one affected part but all around.
2. Experience the pleasure. Enjoy the good feeling that surrounds your new goals and commit yourself to making it a permanent part of your life. Make time in each day to think about the pleasures change confers.

℞3: Make big changes in big things.

To dramatically turn your life around, you've got to change the most important things in your life in the most important ways personally possible. Here's a plan that blueprints the way:

1. Set priorities. Take a careful look at each of the areas you have identified for change. Ask yourself, Is this something I must do now or can it wait? Mentally rank them in priority order—the "musts" taking precedence over the "can waits." Number one on your list is your biggest opportunity to build personal power.
2. Make sure one of the bigger things you do is pay attention to small things. You must never overlook even a minor problem associated with the changes you want. Go out of your way to set things right. Even if you cannot solve it right away, at least it is in your consciousness. Do not forget that power is a cruel master: If you don't do everything right, it will whip you.

℞4: Be the engine of your own deliverance.

Before you can create change, you've got to commit to two important principles of power building:

1. Change isn't an option. It's not something that ought to happen or could happen. It must be something that you feel has to happen.
2. You are in charge. Nobody else can make changes in your life. You must see yourself as the source of change and do what is in your power to make it happen.

By taking full and complete responsibility for creating change you automatically control your mental, emotional, physical, financial, and work-related destinies.

Today's Assignment

Today's work is to realize, in one simple but powerful exercise, the self-confidence you have built through the pages of this book.

1. Think about some aspect of your life that worries you. It can be emotional, physical, work-related, or social. The important thing is to feel its impact on your life.
2. Dream up what you'd rather feel.
3. Figure out how to get it.
4. Do what you can, in this moment, to make your dream come true.

How to Win People Over

Welcome to the last day of this book . . . and the first day of the rest of your life. It has been my privilege to be your coach through these pages, and I know you've learned a lot about how to deal with people with power and confidence. But as I have emphasized all along, merely knowing something is not enough. You must have a plan—call it a roadmap—to actively practice your strengths, overcome your weaknesses, and consistently produce over time the dramatic and lasting improvements you desire and deserve.

Self-Test: Rate Your New Ability to Win People Over

In closing, I am going to repeat an earlier self-test. The idea is to compare your present results with earlier ones. From this comparison comes your lifetime plan to win people over at home, on the job, and out in the community.

Below, I have listed fourteen subjects related to the acquisition and practice of power. Beneath each is a scale from 1 to 10. I want you to read each topic, think about it for a moment. Then, I'd like you to rate your ability in each specific area. Just circle the number that, in your judgment, reflects your level of skill. The lower the number you assign, the weaker your ability in the area. Try to avoid the highest and lowest numbers unless you think an area deserves an extreme mark.

1. Getting others to respect your intelligence.

   Weak *Strong*

   1...2...3...4...5...6...7...8...9...10

2. Making your ideas their ideas.
   Weak *Strong*
   1...2...3...4...5...6...7...8...9...10
3. Making failure an impossibility.
   Weak *Strong*
   1...2...3...4...5...6...7...8...9...10
4. Handling difficult people.
   Weak *Strong*
   1...2...3...4...5...6...7...8...9...10
5. Overcoming a bad situation constructively.
   Weak *Strong*
   1...2...3...4...5...6...7...8...9...10
6. Getting what you want even when you are only half right.
   Weak *Strong*
   1...2...3...4...5...6...7...8...9...10
7. Getting ahead without getting stabbed in the back.
   Weak *Strong*
   1...2...3...4...5...6...7...8...9...10
8. Leveraging office politics to get ahead.
   Weak *Strong*
   1...2...3...4...5...6...7...8...9...10
9. Winning instant acceptance from your peers.
   Weak *Strong*
   1...2...3...4...5...6...7...8...9...10
10. Overcoming a poor reputation.
    Weak *Strong*
    1...2...3...4...5...6...7...8...9...10

11. Getting back on the good side of others when a relationship has been damaged.

Weak *Strong*

1...2...3...4...5...6...7...8...9...10

12. Preventing the stress of your job from getting to you.

Weak *Strong*

1...2...3...4...5...6...7...8...9...10

13. Enlisting your boss's help to go after your boss's job.

Weak *Strong*

1...2...3...4...5...6...7...8...9...10

14. Being the master of change and not its victim.

Weak *Strong*

1...2...3...4...5...6...7...8...9...10

Now that you have completed the exercise, simply compare your present results to those you recorded on pages 149 and 150.

Pay special attention to those areas where little or no positive change shows up. These represent areas where added effort is likely to bring the most dramatic shifts in power and self-confidence. If you will concentrate on these as you move forward, you cannot possibly fail to overcome the weaknesses that are keeping you from getting what you want out of life.

I sincerely hope the time we've spent together brings you the personal and business rewards that come from dealing with people with power and confidence.

We've never met face to face but, as I leave you now, I want you to know how much I admire and respect you as a person. You've given me the privilege of working side by side with you to share my skills, and my sincere hope is that these touch your life in a special way.

Index